The Divine Spark

Second Edition

We are all one.

Carri Hoagland

*The first principle of Judaism
teaches us all human beings
are created in the divine image and
therefore are linked to God by the
Divine Spark within them.*

The Divine Spark

Personal Stories of LGBTQ Discovery

Second Edition

The Divine Spark

Copyright 2018 and 2024 by Nancy Hanson
All rights reserved. Printed in the U.S.A.
Pages of this book may be photocopied.
Printed by PFLAG Washburn, Washburn, Wisconsin
ISBN: 979-8-9899092-1-6

Second Edition

Editorial assistance by Philip J. Sorensen
Cover art by G. Scott Hanson
Book design by Copy That, Ashland, Wisconsin
Book printing by Smartpress, Chanhassen, Minnesota

*This book is dedicated
to the brave and vulnerable
writers of each chapter.*

Contents

Foreword	Corinne Chilstrom	*iii*
Introduction to the Second Edition	Nancy Hanson	*ii*
Who Are You [poem]	John Berton	*vii*
The Times, They Are a-Changin'	Keith Holm	1
Two-Spirited = Androgynous	Dianne M. Heapy	15
Here I Am: Fourteen and Gay	Sorley Swanstrom-Arnold	23
Arriving at Peace	Anonymous	27
Thirty Seconds Plus	Brian Henning	32
Shoulders	Yolanda Denson-Byers	37
I Feel Like a Woman	Carri Hoagland	43
Acceptance	Anonymous	49
Odyssey to Kindness	Stephanie Winter	53
Will You Love the You You Hide?	Jason Clifton	61
I am Episcopalian, a Priest, and Gay	Mark Ricker	65
The McGregors are Queers	Anonymous	71
Freak Out to Peace Out	Katie Makolondra	73
Divine Favor	Michael Van Uytven	79
My Sister, My Brother	Niki Pohnl	83
Love Conquers All	Mary Bondeson	87
Fathom	Jeanne Clark	93
Mama Bear	Kate Stolp	101
Grace Upon Grace	Dale Chesley	105
God's Justice, God's Love	Nate Aaseng	113
The Next Step	Aubrey Thonvold	117

Resources 119
History of PFLAG Washburn 126
PFLAG Overview 129
What PFLAG Stands For 131
Introduction to the First Edition 134
Epilogue from the First Edition 136
Acknowledgements 139
How to Purchase The Divine Spark 141

i

The Divine Spark

Foreword

from the First Edition, 2018

by Corinne Chilstrom

These authors form a common bond as they come to us, sharing their lives. Rejection began at a young age, simply for being born LGBTQ through no choice of their own. As teens, troubled by their own same gender attraction or gender non-conformity, they began hearing condemnation loud and clear, from both church and the broader society. Their stories pull at your heart strings as they render authentic accounts of what happened to them.

Those most hardened against LGBTQ people believe they chose their lifestyle. If only they would "confess it as sin" or "get counseling," they could be restored to a "normal, straight life."

But stay with their stories and your defenses will crumble. You will see real individual souls who have carried, often secretively and alone, heavy burdens few could have endured.

So, dear reader, we invite you to relax, take in these stories with an open heart and mind. Unmask your own core, same as these "neighbors we have from God" have unmasked themselves.

God's Spirit will move you to help the LGBTQ community, to stand up for them and advocate for their justice.

God bless you as you ponder these stories from the very essence of people who long for acceptance. May your heart receive them openly, with the doing God requires. Listen to the prophet Micah from so long ago: "What does the Lord require of you, but to do justice, and to love kindness, and to walk humbly with your God," Micah 6:8 (NRSV).

Corinne Chilstrom, retired Evangelical Lutheran Church in America (ELCA) pastor, and Herb Chilstrom, retired presiding bishop of the ELCA, both in their eighties, reside in Arizona. They are forever touched by the loss of their son Andrew, a freshman at Gustavus Adolphus College, who took his life on November 11, 1984. In 1993 Corinne wrote Andrew, You Died Too Soon, A Family Experience of Grieving and Living Again. *Herb's book,* When A Father Loses A Son *came out in 2017. Rev. Dr. Herbert Chilstrom died in 2020.*

Introduction
to the Second Edition

Greetings and salutations, everyone!

We first published this book in 2018. As copies of the first printing started to dwindle, PFLAG Washburn Volunteer Executive Director Kate Stolp noted, "*The Divine Spark* remains popular at our various events. The book gives voice to those who struggle with negative religious views of the LGBTQ community." Kate applied for a grant to print more copies.

Tamarack Health Ashland Medical Center granted PFLAG Washburn the funding necessary to print the second edition of *The Divine Spark,* as well as the new book *The Little Book of Love from the Chequamegon Bay and Beyond.*

After learning of the grant, we decided to make a few revisions rather than reprint without changes. Jeanne Clark and Kate Stolp gave us two new stories from a parental perspective. Yolanda Denson-Byers and Michael Van Uytven wrote about being queer and Christian. Sorley Swanstrom-Arnold, Carri Hoagland, and Keith Holm added to their original stories. We also expanded our resource guide.

When reading Keith's update, you may be struck by his plea for all of us to focus on love and faith instead of fear and blame. Native Choctaw theologian and Episcopal Bishop Steven Charleston describes a similar view of fear and hope in his book *We Survived the End of the World*:

The Divine Spark

> ... [R]enewal and reconciliation for all life remained at the center of what motivated hope in the hearts of Native people. The roots of fear run deep. The hope we embrace must run just as deep. No matter what happens we must keep dancing, hand in hand, joined in a circle of equality, constantly moving in the slow rotation of justice and prayer... [W]e must be dedicated to a vision and willing to dance for it for as long as it takes. That level of commitment... is necessary if we are to diminish the apocalypse we see rising before us.

An apocalypse indeed rises before us. States continue to enact legislation which tries to kill the divine spark in our LGBTQ siblings. Especially this year, we have a duty to stand up and speak out. Please read about PFLAG on pages 126-133.

Share *The Divine Spark* stories, join PFLAG or any other open and affirming organization, band together to support, educate and advocate. Everyone deserves an equal chance to let their light shine.

Aloha,

Nancy Hanson

PFLAG Washburn founding board member and retired pastor

February, 2024

The Introduction to the First Edition (2018) starts on page 134.

Who Are You

by John Berton

Being gay is not like
being a Democrat or a Republican
it is not like
being a Christian, Muslim or Jew
it is not like
deciding to buy a BMW, VCR and condo in Lincoln Park
it is not like
voting for Ross Perot or having vanilla instead of
chocolate ice cream on that slice of pecan pie

Being gay is not a lifestyle. It is not a choice. It is like
Being Black or Asian or White or
Being 5'6" or 6'5" or
Being blue-eyed or brown-eyed

It is like having one arm, or two or
being a woman or a man or
seeing with two eyes or perhaps none

It is not something that can be changed.

Being gay is part of
BEING who you ARE

It is a discovery

© 1993, John Berton

The Times, They Are a-Changin'

Come mothers and fathers all over the land
Don't criticize what you can't understand
Your sons and your daughters are beyond your command
For the times they are a-changin'.

– Bob Dylan

by Keith Holm

2018 Original Essay

When I was a senior in high school these lyrics were part of a four-minute speech I delivered at a state forensics meet in Wisconsin. I surprised myself by getting an A. Times were changing in the late sixties and early seventies. The war in Vietnam was coming to an end. Young people were becoming activists and love was free. Except for me.

I knew at an early age I was different from my playmates. They would look at pictures of women in bras and panties in the JC Penney catalogue. I'd look at the men's underwear models. As I grew older I finally figured out I was gay, or to use the term of the day, queer. I knew being queer was wrong, that queers were picked on, bullied and often beat up. I wanted none of that. But I could not help who I was.

My parents took me to church on Sundays. I went to Sunday school and confirmation. It was here when I first heard being queer is a sin and queer people will be damned. Heaven was not for me. I heard it over and over in church. I heard it at home. I heard it from friends who did not know I was one of "those" people. I felt my only hope was to keep my feelings to myself and just get on with my life. My secret life.

My parents, God love them, had no clue about homosexuality. They didn't know any gay people and as good Christians no doubt my parents would have felt it their duty to change homosexuals, to pray the gay away. I wondered for a long time if I could be fixed somehow. Maybe God would make my feelings go away.

It never happened.

I concluded God did not exist. I still went to church with my family when I was a kid. I would sit there during the service hoping God would keep my secret and make sure my parents would never find out. I could not imagine how disappointed they would be if they knew their "little boy" was queer, so I continued to hide my homosexuality.

At age 29 I moved to St. Paul, Minnesota. I had a great job in a very conservative organization. I needed to keep my secret at the workplace for sure. There were no laws protecting LGBT people from discrimination in jobs and housing. No big deal, I thought. I was getting good at living and organizing my life in the closet.

One day after answering phones for a telethon in Minneapolis, I decided to walk down the street and go into the Gay 90s bar. I had never been there before. I knew it as the biggest gay bar in The Cities. I was scared to death, but went in anyway. I sat at one of the bars and ordered a drink. A diverse crowd packed the place. Men of all ages and sizes. When I emptied my glass, the bartender brought me another drink and said, "It's on that guy over there." He pointed across the bar. Oh, no. Now what? Who sent the drink? I didn't know what to do.

I remembered my manners and called the bartender over. I asked him to send a drink to the person who had bought one for me. The bartender made a drink, walked to the other side of the bar, and put it down in front of a young, incredibly handsome man. I about fell off my stool. The rest, as they say, is history.

Paul and I spent the evening together. I never believed in love at first sight, but it happened to us that night. He was 21. I was 31. For the very first time, I felt love. Real love. It felt great. We were incredibly happy.

We moved in together about a month later. Life was good.

What am I going to do about my family? I told myself I would never come out to my family unless or until I met someone I wanted to spend the rest of my life with. I knew they would go crazy. I would be kicked out of the family, taken out of the will, and would never see them again. But I was prepared for it. I met the man I wanted to spend the rest of my life with.

Mom and Dad came to visit in St. Paul fairly often. Paul was introduced as my "roommate." They bought it for a while.

The first New Year's Eve they spent with us, we put a cot in the master bedroom so Mom and Dad could stay in Paul's room.

After dinner Paul started clearing the table and cleaning the kitchen. Mom offered to help, but Paul said no. He wanted her to relax and enjoy the evening. For the next year we visited Mom and Dad up north at the cottage. It was fine. We had separate beds.

The next New Year's Eve, Mom and Dad were back in St. Paul. We had a great dinner. When we finished, Paul started doing his thing, his thing being the kitchen. He hated it when someone offered to help clean the kitchen, because no one could do it as well as he could. Mom again offered to help, and Paul said, "No, thank you." She picked up some dishes and headed to the kitchen anyway. He thanked mom, but escorted her to the family room. They went home the next day. Whew, we thought. We pulled it off again.

A few days later my sister Barb called. She told me mom and dad asked her if we were gay. Nobody else would be so fussy about his kitchen. Paul must be gay! My sister had known for years I was gay, but she always kept my secret. Barb wanted to know what to tell them. I told her to go ahead and tell them.

The next morning the call came.

"Are you gay?"

Long pause.

"Yes," I said.

As expected, all of the horrible things I thought would happen, or would be said, did happen and were said.

My mom thought the devil had taken up residence in my house.

I was in my car driving to a meeting, so I pulled off the freeway into a parking lot and listened to them rant and rave for fifteen minutes.

We finally said "good-bye." I knew it would be for life. I cried my eyes out, turned the car around, and went home to my partner, my rock. He had a horrible coming out experience with his family a few years earlier, so he knew what I was feeling and what I was going though.

"We will get through this," he said.

And we did.

About six months later Mom and Dad finally called and asked if they could come up for the weekend. Their words stunned me. We hadn't spoken a word since that fateful phone call.

We all spent the evening together having dinner and watching TV. The first night they slept in their camper in the driveway. The next day the four of us went sightseeing and hit the supermarket sample tables, which my dad loved. That evening mom asked if they could spend the night in the freshly named guest room. It was the beginning of a new relationship for our family.

Over the years Paul and I always felt they liked him more than me. Mom loved how he took such good care of me. In fact the whole conservative, God fearing family became quite fond of Paul. They loved him and loved that the two of us were together.

This book is about helping LGBTQ people know they remain beloved children of God. I struggled with such a notion for a long time. I could not get the words of my childhood pastor out of my head, him preaching heaven was not for me, nor for us. But how could that be? I did not believe in God, yet thought God must exist because how else could I explain my great fortune to have such a wonderful man as Paul in my life? I thought it might be a good idea to start working on exploring our spiritual life together. We tried a couple churches. One was too gay for us. The others we tried felt unwelcoming. We gave up.

About five years after we met, Paul started having some health issues so we finally decided to get the AIDS test. We would go together. No one wanted to get tested because in those days you could lose your job, housing, insurance, nearly everything. But I said we needed to do it.

Paul's test came back positive. I was negative.

For the next four years we rode the medical roller coaster of living with AIDS. Paul was in and out of the hospital. We lived by the numbers. T cell counts. Blood counts. There was only one drug available at the time. AZT became our greatest hope. AIDS finally obliterated Paul's immune system and he developed liver and throat cancer. On the 3rd of March, 1993 at 12:45 a.m., Paul's battle came to an end.

Paul passed away at home, his mom and I by his side. There was no sound. He simply stopped breathing. I knew this day would come and thought I would be ready for it. I was not. My heart was broken. My life partner gone. It scared me to think what would happen next. Would we ever be together again? Does God exist? Is heaven real? How could God let this happen?

We sat there in silence. I could hear the words of my confirmation pastor in my head. Queer people will be damned. I felt sick to my stomach.

That's when it happened. There were no words spoken. No vision or beam of light. A feeling came over me unlike anything I had ever felt. I suddenly felt warm inside. I felt like I had invisible arms around me, holding me close. I felt safe. I felt love unlike any love I had ever felt before. I will never forget it as long as I live. The feeling was indescribable. Then it was gone.

Later that day, I asked Paul's mother if she felt anything shortly after Paul passed. She described exactly the same feeling.

That night I became a believer. God touched my soul and my heart. God let me know Paul was with Him and we would be together again. He let me know Paul was loved. He let me know I was loved. And His love was unconditional. I received an amazing gift. God's love is for everyone.   It doesn't make any difference if you are gay, straight, transgender or anything on the spectrum. God took away my fear of death that night. When my time comes I will not be afraid. I will look forward to meeting God and reuniting with my partner and family and friends who have gone before me. They wait for me. I know it.

A couple months after Paul passed, I spent the weekend with my parents. As we drove to the grocery store, Mom asked me how I was doing. Then she said, "There will never be anyone like Paul. Nobody will ever take care of you like he did." These words were coming from the woman who called him the "devil" years earlier.

She went into the store leaving Dad and me in the car. Dad started to cry.

"What's wrong?" I asked.

Dad said, "I am so very sorry I wasn't there for you and made you hide your life from us."

It astonished me to hear these words from my parents. God performed a miracle with my family. It's what God does. God can perform one for you too.

It has been quite a ride. I am now 65 years old. After Paul passed, I dated from time to time. I met lots of interesting people, but none came close to him. I am still single, although Pastor Nancy keeps trying to set me up. Life is good. I moved to Washburn, Wisconsin and joined Messiah Lutheran Church. I was a little worried about being out in such a small community. As it happened, I didn't need to worry at all.

When the church considered adopting a policy allowing the pastor to marry same-gender couples, even before gay marriage became the law of the land, one member of our committee did not like the idea. He knew me from church, but did not know I was gay. During the course of discussion, I let the committee know the importance of the policy to me and to my fellow LGBT members of the community. It was essential for our church to welcome everyone and for LGBT people to feel safe in our church and community. I had outed myself to the committee, specifically, to Clayton.

At first, my friend Clayton referred to gays as "those people" during the meetings. He did not intend to be derogatory. I wondered if perhaps I was the first gay person he knew. Nonetheless, the recommendation to approve a gay marriage policy passed unanimously, largely because of Clayton's support.

One Sunday after church my new friend Clayton asked whether I would give him a ride downtown. Before he got out of the car, he asked me if I liked country music and if I liked a drink at happy hour. I told him I liked both. He told me I should stop over sometime. "Keith, you will always be welcome in my home."

It was an amazing moment. I am so glad we shared it together.

> *Come mothers and fathers all over the land*
> *Don't criticize what you can't understand*
> *Your sons and your daughters are beyond your command*
> *For the times they are a-changin'.*

As I think back on Dylan's lyrics and reflect on my personal growth as a gay man and my personal growth with God, I would have to agree that indeed the times, they are a-changin'.

When I was young no support groups, hot lines, or LGBTQ organizations existed. No PFLAG. No gay friendly congregations. We have come a long way. But we have a long way to go. If you are a young person struggling with your identity, don't give up. My story and countless others' prove how much goodness endures in the world and how people can change.

You deserve to live your life as you, and to love whom you want to love. You will run into people who won't like you very much. You will hear people who have "SBI" (Selective Biblical Interpretationitis). They will tell you being gay is a sin. Pay no attention to them. God's love is for everyone. Dylan's words still ring true. People are changing. People are becoming more and more understanding and accepting. I can say without hesitation or reservation God loves us just as we are.

Be strong!

2024 Essay

I no longer live in Washburn, Wisconsin. In 2020 I gave up the freezing winters and moved to Tucson, Arizona. I live in a community of townhomes on a golf course (I don't golf) with spectacular views of Pusch Ridge and the Catalina Mountains. I am blessed with wonderful, caring neighbors, each of whom received a copy of *The Divine Spark*. I felt it was the best way for them to get to know me and my life. When they finished reading my story there were hugs and some tears. I was welcomed into a new community of conservatives and liberals without judgement. We have come a long way indeed.

The year 2023 marked the 30th anniversary of my partner Paul's death. I still have favorite pictures of him in my home including his baby picture given to me by his mom. I look at those pictures, then look at me and wonder what the hell happened? I see a 71-year-old man complete with all the aches and pains that come with life and then I look at his picture. He's still young. Still handsome. Still missed every day.

I wrote that Paul had a terrible coming-out experience with his family. Here is more of his story. Paul knew at an early age he was gay. He also knew his parents would not accept having a gay son. When he was a senior in high school he had a brief relationship with a fellow classmate, in secret, of course. If you've ever lived in a small town, one thing you know for sure is there are no secrets. Paul's secret got out. His parents kicked him out of the house. He had enough credits to graduate, but suddenly found himself on the street. He was 17.

I could never understand how that could happen. How two parents who loved their son and cared for him could suddenly turn their love off and throw him from the only home he ever knew. I don't get it. I still don't. And yet it happens every day to gay and transgender kids.

Paul was flat broke and on the street. He found his way to Minneapolis where he did what he needed to survive. He made friends easily and was offered places to stay while he went to dental assistant school. Shortly after he got kicked out of his home, Paul received a call from his uncle who invited him to come over to the house. He wanted to *talk* things over. When Paul arrived at the fancy west-metro home, the *talk* quickly went south. His uncle beat him bloody. There would be no gays in the family, period! Paul had enough cash to take a bus up to his grandparents' house in Duluth. Paul stayed there until he healed up and was well enough to go back to school and work. His grandparents helped as much as they could. Paul was dead to the rest of his family. After a while Paul and his mother reconciled a bit. I don't know how he did it. They had been so very cruel. But that was Paul.

When we met, Paul was living alone in a third-floor studio apartment in the Loring Park area of Minneapolis. He had recently ended a relationship. I was happy things had not worked out, for I stumbled into the love of my life in a gay bar in downtown Minneapolis.

Our early years together presented plenty of challenges. Paul had been badly damaged throughout his life by the people around him who put Paul down for being gay. Nearly everyone he loved berated him. His self-esteem lay in tatters. He had no self-confidence whatsoever. I'd invite friends over to the house and he would either leave or go to bed early. The shame he felt broke my heart, but we worked on it. We worked on it together by talking about it. We shared the same shame. The same guilt. My job forced me to deal with it. I had a choice to make. While at work, I had to set my shame aside. It worked for me professionally. It also worked for me because I had Paul to talk to when I got home. And he had me. It took a few years, but he finally came around and felt proud of his life and the life we had created together.

In this book's first release, I did not write about the years of roller coaster rides from one health crisis to another. I did not write about our first hospital visit in Minneapolis where staff would leave food on the floor outside his room. That experience was jarring and humiliating. I hated Paul's doctor, who basically gave up on Paul. I hated the uneducated, paranoid staff for their dreadful care. Paul and I lasted there two days while I researched and found him a new infectious disease specialist in St. Paul. We checked into United Hospital in St. Paul the next day. What a difference good care makes. We rode the health care roller coaster for five years. I would hop on the same ride again in a minute if I could have more time with my beloved Paul.

During the last couple months of Paul's life, his family started coming out of the woodwork. It shocked them to discover Paul and

I had been together for almost ten years; that we had a great life together; that we lived in a beautiful home on the bluffs overlooking St Paul; that my family and friends loved Paul and they loved us as a couple.

So, one by one, they visited.

Paul pretty much stayed on the flop-out couch in the living room during his final days. His mother was with us most weekdays when I was working. Her care shift ended when I got home from work. Paul's mom told us that one of her brothers wanted to come visit. It was one of the brothers who banished Paul from the family. Yet, Paul was thrilled. He quickly called and invited his uncle and his girlfriend to come for the weekend. They did. Then Paul's brother came. He visited a few times, even bringing his wife and kids once. Paul was thrilled. Then the uncle who had beat the shit out of Paul came by with his wife. I'm not sure if Paul was thrilled or not, but I seethed trying to welcome him into our home. But for Paul, I did it. I opened our home to the hateful homophobe. So many family members looking for absolution tried to pay their respects to Paul one last time before he died. They wanted absolution from the heartless and spiteful treatment of their brother, nephew, and son. Paul gave them exactly what they came looking for. He gave them absolution.

As for me, I will let God make that call.

About a week after Paul died, I got a letter from the wife of the uncle who beat Paul. She apologized for everything. It was a beautiful, heartfelt letter. I wonder if her husband ever saw it.

I came home one day about a week before Paul passed to find a strange car in the driveway. I went inside. The living room was empty, but there was a strong smell of burning grass or leaves. Then I heard voices in the basement. Paul had invited a Greek Orthodox priest to come to the house for blessings. Paul dragged the priest all over the house blessing pretty much everything in sight. From my basement workshop to the washer and dryer I loathed (Paul did all the laundry), to the TV, guest room, the dog, and finally, me. The priest was very thorough. Though our spiritual life may have been lacking, we do what we need to do to connect with our Maker when death becomes imminent. Both of us wanted and needed the spiritual connection, and we got it.

So here we are. It's 2024. I just spent my thirtieth Christmas alone living with wonderful memories of the many Christmases we shared. Paul loved Christmas. One year we had five trees in the house. It took me ten years after Paul died to put up another tree. A good friend lost her husband to cancer this year and she remains devastated. I feel her pain in her every post. When last we talked, I told her I wished I could tell her the pain will go away. It won't. I still feel it thirty years later. But we learn to live with it. We get strength from our memories. We have taken a big step when those memories bring smiles instead of tears.

"The times they are a changing." Prophetic words then and now. I have watched all my 71 years on earth the progress the LGBTQ community has made. The high point was the Supreme Court decision to make same sex marriage the law of the land. We could feel the winds of equality sweeping the country. Then we started seeing hate. We live in a very different world today. It has become sport in politics to create fear in people and then claim to be the only one with a solution. Blame the gays for your lot in life. Blame transgender kids. Blame immigrants. Blame women who want the right to make decisions on their own healthcare. Blame books. Blame Disney. Scare the hell out of people.

Placing blame or scaring people solves nothing. The solution lies in loving each other. Don't take away rights, expand them. Don't burn books, encourage people to read them.

The Divine Spark

Do you know someone who is gay or trans? Walk in their shoes for a while. Feel the pain they feel when they are told they don't belong or that they are somehow broken. I learned years ago it's a lot easier to hate than it is to love. Love takes work. Love takes caring, understanding, and empathy. And love takes faith.

I have been dealing with prostate cancer since 2016 and cannot predict what lies ahead. I've gone through surgery, radiation, hormone therapy, and immunotherapy. Most recently I had something called a lymphadenectomy to remove some positive lymph nodes. As I continue my fight against cancer, I remain the eternal optimist. I am not planning on checking out anytime soon, but when my time comes, the experience I had on March 3rd, 1993, gives me faith that Paul and I will be together again. When I meet new people who ask me about my life or about my past, I give them a copy of *The Divine Spark*. My story is here. My hope is here in these pages.

Keith Holm, 2016-2017 Messiah Lutheran Church Council President, retired to Washburn, Wisconsin after a 29-year career as the chief executive officer of the St. Paul Area Association of Realtors. Tired of Wisconsin winters, Keith moved to Tucson, Arizona in 2020.

Two-Spirited = Androgynous

has other meanings, too!

We fell in love with a person, not a gender or an ideology, and certainly not a label.

– Ellen Hart

by Dianne M. Heapy

I have walked as a two-spirited, androgynous person throughout my life. I did not know those terms when I was young. My life has been a spiritual journey with times of pain. Yet today I walk in contentment with the very essence and totality as a two-spirited person.

Spiritual life and faith have been the most important parts of my life since early childhood. Writing this brief autobiography has been emotionally difficult. I am grateful, however, for the opportunity to provide it for others.

"What is the purpose of this story?" Sharing my life experience might save one life, as my life was saved by my high school coach and gymnastics teacher. I was taught the only right way to be, according to society and the church community, was heterosexual. All other ways were a mistake or a sin.

During early childhood I experienced a sense of belonging with my family, and when in school and church. I eventually came to believe I did not belong – anywhere. Now I know I do belong and those teachings were wrong. I was misled.

I am okay just as I am, a two-spirited person. I was born perfectly unique, same as you, same as everyone, just as we are.

My early years filled me with happiness. I lived in Royal Oak, Michigan, a Detroit suburb, surrounded by cousins, aunts and uncles, and my grandparents. We were second generation German Americans with a Cherokee Indian great-great grandmother. I spent a lot of time with my Grandma Bauer. I remember us laughing about the old car she drove as we went places together. She liked the song "Blue Moon." I attended a Missouri Synod Lutheran parochial school during my 2nd and 3rd grade years. Church was important in our family life.

I envied my brother when he received a train set for Christmas one year. I yearned for such a wonderful toy. Instead, I got dolls because I was a girl. But, I did not like the girl toys. I did love climbing trees and being outdoors.

At eight years of age my life changed forever. My family moved to a small, southern Ohio, retired, farming town near the Bible belt. African Americans and other minorities were legally banned from the streets and sidewalks after sundown. The town was steeped in old money and an unspoken hierarchy of social class. Society viewed my family as lower middle class.

I began fourth grade in a segregated public school. Only white children attended. All students in each grade were divided into classes based on their grade point average, except for the isolated mentally disabled. I spoke differently because of my northern roots in Michigan. I had difficulty understanding my teacher because of her more southern, Kentucky accent.

Two-Spirited = Androgynous

I spent my weekends and summer days hiking the trails and levees and fishing the streams by the Miami River. I experienced an emotional and spiritual closeness with the trees, rocks, animals, earth, and sky. I purchased flowers, such as morning glories, and planted them in our small backyard. I liked mowing the lawn, biking, and exploring places such as the vacant old house near the housing development. Many Indian tribes had once lived in Ohio and I enjoyed reading about Indian life because the Native Americans honored all of creation and their spirituality fascinated me. Life during the summers felt good. I dreaded the end of summer and the return to school.

I have fragmented memories of the years in public school. I experienced severe bullying, name-calling, and ridicule. Other students did not include or accept me.

By high school, though a star athlete, I was suicidal. I attempted to end my life by slitting my wrists. I craved death.

My coach spent many hours talking with me when I did not have the words or comprehension of what made my life so awful. Even though I could not identify or express the thoughts and feelings of why I wanted to die, she listened to me. She compassionately talked with me about many things, including God's love for me, and that I existed as a unique, special person.

I finally met a friend. She became my girlfriend during my sophomore year of high school. We spent much of our time together, even though we lived a distance from each other. We had a physical relationship and I loved her. While I felt loved and accepted by her, I nevertheless continued to struggle with loving and accepting myself.

So I read the Bible, especially Romans. I listened to the pastor and heard my mother say things like, "If you just dressed and acted more like a girl, boys would be interested in you." I felt condemned by the Apostle Paul's writings. I kept trying to fit in and be accepted by anyone as their friend, and accepted and loved by my parents. Most of all I wanted to feel welcomed and loved by the church people, the pastor, and Jesus, who supposedly loved me because "the Bible told me so."

I graduated from high school refusing to recognize God loved me, but I knew my girlfriend loved me. We discussed how we could do life together forever. After our high school graduation, we took separate paths. My girlfriend attended a school of nursing in Ohio and I entered a Deaconess program at a Lutheran college in Minnesota. At Christmas that year my girlfriend told me her mother had found a letter she had written to me. Her mother discussed with her the awfulness and shamefulness of our homosexual relationship. My girlfriend ended the relationship by saying she had a boyfriend and would never see me again.

The following school year I met with a college chaplain and confessed my same sex relationship. He wanted me to leave the college immediately. He said I represented a threat to other women in the dorms. Eventually I left the school feeling unloved by God, unforgiven by God and the chaplain, and rejected not only by others, but also by Jesus. The childhood song says, "Jesus, loves me, this I know." I asked myself, "Where is this Jesus?"

I did not know who I was. I did not know where I belonged, and I could not understand why I felt so different from other women. I wanted to be anyone but me.

I kept trying to reconnect with the God of my childhood – the joy of family, the love and joy I experienced with God's people. I began attending an Episcopal Church while holding down a job at a large city bank, and also partying and "running with" the Dayton, Ohio chapter of The Outlaws, a motorcycle gang. It was the '60s and

Two-Spirited = Androgynous

I used drugs, drank hard alcohol, and partied when I wasn't working. I did not want to feel or think. Mainly, I did not want to be me.

"God, why did you create me this way, a woman who is different, considered damaged, sinful, and doesn't belong anywhere?" I asked.

My church said I could be released only through the transforming power of Jesus. To be free I simply needed to deal with the sin of homosexuality. Confess and repent. I could become "truly a new creature in Christ." Yet I had tried confessing, I tried repenting, and I felt only rejection by God even more than before.

What I did not know, but can see clearly now, was that God, Sacred Spirit, has always been with me. Sacred Spirit expressed love and acceptance to me through the times of understanding and discussions of Jesus's love by my high school coach. Sacred Spirit kept me safe during the years with the Outlaws while using drugs and alcohol. Sacred Spirit protected me during an attempted sexual assault while babysitting during my teen years. Spirit guided me with words, gentleness, and love given by a faithful community. Above all, the Sacred Presence gave me "aha" moments when I would see and experience clearly as God, the Sacred Spirit, spoke to me.

Later in life a two-spirited Ojibwe woman became my life partner. I learned from her that I am also two-spirited which explains why the spiritual and healing events have always been so important to me. In Native American culture many two-spirited people are healers, visionaries, dreamers, and keepers of the traditions. My sexuality has been only part of my life journey. My spiritual walk with Great Spirit/God represents the walk, the journey. It is because of Great Spirit, the God and Goddess of all creation, I am alive today.

Years ago I asked my partner for a copy of *Rolling Thunder* for my birthday. I received a copy of it with a card inscribed,

> *You said you would like a copy of this book for your very own.*
> *Here it is. It is your very own with all my love.*
> *And may the Spirit of Rolling Thunder be with you always. Y*
> *ou, your spirit, is truly Indian.*
> *Giving you this book as a birthday gift is my pleasure.*
> *I love you.*

Even though I have experienced pain and loss, I now am able to see love has truly blessed my life journey. In my reading of the Bible, the following bullet points illustrate what Spirit has shown me and what I would like to share with LGBTQ members growing up in Christian churches:

- God/Goddess is the totality of human sexuality as indicated by the empty seat on the Ark of the Covenant. It is not empty. God, the totality of all sexuality, sits upon it.
- I am, and you are, created in the image of God, the Goddess, Great Spirit. We are all descendants of the Sacred, thus our uniqueness is a Sacredness passed down through the ages, by our ancestors, beginning with God, Great Spirit, the Parent of all of us.
- We are loved and accepted just as Spirit created us in Sacred Spirit image – gay, lesbian, bisexual, transgender, queer. Spirit has made us and brought us into the world, just as we are. We were known "before the creation of the world," (Ephesians1:4). "Before I formed you in the womb, I knew you," (Jeremiah 1:5).
- We were dedicated and known by Sacred Spirit before we were born, just as we came into the world at birth," (Jeremiah 1:4).

Paraphrasing Paul in his letter to the Corinthians:

> *The journey of knowing the very essence of who I am, I now understand as 'having seen my sexual identity clearly, me, as only an unknown*

reflection in a mirror in my youth. But now I see face to face the totality of me. I only knew in part as I was aging, but I now know fully, even as I have always been fully known by God as I am.'

What I did not know and had not been taught or shown by others was "I was fully known" always by a loving Father/Spirit. We were sent into the world, just as we are, just as God/Sacred Spirit made us to be in the world. And no one can take this away from us – ever.

A mental health professional, Dianne M. Heapy worked in the Chequamegon Bay area for quality of life for all people. Now retired, she moved to Little Canada, Minnesota in 2021 to be closer to family.

Kids' mental health in Wisconsin
is not only on the decline, but may
be at a new all-time low.
That's according to a new report
out on January 12, 2024.
The Wisconsin Office of Children's
Mental Health 2023 report says
there has been a large increase in
young adults with any mental illness.
Another startling discovery:
half of LGBTQ+ youth in the state
are considering suicide.

"Youth Mental Health Declining in Wisconsin"
ABC WXOW.com News 19 • January 12, 2024

Here I Am: Fourteen and Gay

by Sorley Swanstrom-Arnold

2018 ORIGINAL ESSAY

My name is Sorley Swanstrom-Arnold. I am fourteen years old and I am gay. Coming out as gay nowadays is far easier than it was when my parents were in high school. I am, fortunately, not under constant threat of physical abuse or teasing. In addition, the Internet can make it easier to come out. I, for example, exploded out of the closet with a Snapchat post and an Instagram picture. I received support from friends in the form of comments saying, "Way to own it dude!," or "So proud of you!"

But coming out did not arrive without its struggles. For a long time I questioned my sexuality. It wasn't until a girl asked me out that I finally came upon my realization. We went on one date and spent some time together. She helped me understand I was in fact gay. Yet it devastated her, and I felt completely responsible for her grief. My sadness, coupled with unrelenting teasing from people I considered friends, led to self-harm.

I was called names like *gay boy* and *fag*. I was afraid to confront these people so I just laughed along. I eventually moved myself out of such a toxic environment and into a more accepting community of people who, like me, were part of the LGBTQ community. We all had our struggles, and having the close connection to similar people helped us through the hardships.

I pushed my way through the self-harm and negative feelings to find myself happy. I had a wonderful group of friends. I was far more outgoing about my sexuality even putting on some makeup here and there. I felt good.

Then came my gender confusion. I have male parts, but I never felt like a "boy." I stood about as far away from masculine as one could get. I felt comfortable wearing makeup. I thought I might look good in a dress, though I never had the chance to try one on. Of course, it went the other way as well. I did not feel like a girl, either.

I struggled with my identity quite a bit during my gender bewilderment. Yet I found my savior in the term "gender queer." I began using they/them pronouns. I took this identity change slower than before, telling only my closest friends. For whatever reason, gender remains a far more sensitive subject than sexuality.

2024 ESSAY

I will be twenty-one in March, 2024 and attend Luther College in Decorah, Iowa. Six years ago I wrote the above piece about my experience as a young queer man. Since then, nearly a third of my life has elapsed (wild), and in those years my relationship with my sexuality and gender have continually changed. I do not solidly define my gender or sexuality like I did last time. I see no use in that now.

Generally, I tend to think of myself as a queer man. I do not think I have any new insights or profound discoveries to describe. My journey has been one of rapid, confusing change. The labels I assign myself have been swapped out so many times I do not find it useful to use them anymore.

Such is my experience, and mine alone.

Sometimes, either unconsciously, or anxiously, I regret the things I wrote six years ago. They describe a person I am not anymore. I acknowledge the uncomfortable feeling to have that record existing in perpetuity. But I do believe – even though my sexual and gender identity have shifted over time and I am not the "same person" as I was back then – it was still me who wrote those words. The experiences I wrote about remain as central to myself as anything. I do not regret or feel ashamed of the changes which have taken place in my life.

In some ways I wish I had profound new advice to share, but I do not. If anything, this is simply a way to add another notation in my journey. Nonetheless, thank you for reading. Thank you for listening. Thank you for accepting.

In 2018 Sorley Swanstrom was a ninth grader at Washburn High School in Washburn, Wisconsin enjoying French class, science, and show choir. Now Sorley is in his third year as a student at Luther College in Decorah, Iowa.

So I was not alone after all.

Others like me existed.

Anonymous

Arriving at Peace

by Anonymous

In all the years of my life, I don't think I have ever doubted the existence of God. I may have doubted myself. I may have wondered at an early age why I had feelings so different from all my other friends. Sometimes, though, a person simply must have faith and belief in their feelings, because there is no one else around who can support and listen to you. Getting to that peace of mind for me, however, meant enduring some frightening experiences.

I grew up in such an insulated environment I did not have any names for what my attraction to men was all about. The Stonewall riots had not yet occurred and on top of that, no resources, whether community or church based, were available to me. Needless to say, a child could not have made an appointment to see a therapist without his parents being made aware of the peculiarities of that discussion.

So peace was a long time coming.

Peace certainly would not have come to our house had I voiced my concerns and questions. My parents, both devout Christians, believed in the literal translation of the Bible. It had to be the King James Version, the version that raised all good Scandinavians. My parents served as pillars of the church, filling volunteer positions, like organist, Sunday school teacher, deacon, singer, vacation Bible school instructor, counselor at summer Bible camp, and fill-in for the pastor in the pulpit when the pastor was on vacation or had been called away on short notice. It was not uncommon for one of our family or the whole family to be found at the church at least three or four times a week. In fact, everyone downright expected we would be there.

But I never felt any rebelliousness. Instead, I thrived, loving the community, basking in the social and spiritual aspects of the church. Living the love. There was a lot of love in our family. We deeply cared for each other on a spiritual, ethical, and daily level. Neighbor helped neighbor. The church in town where we worshiped stood as an important cog in the cultural wheel of our small community. I grew up loving – loving my family, loving God. We never wanted for anything. Life felt wonderful in our little corner of the world.

Not until the 70s brought cultural strides for the civil rights of different groups of people did things start happening for me. I graduated from high school in the early 70s, ready to set foot in the world. I still had security and support from my family, much like all good people who receive their diploma. They say goodbye to their alma mater. They say goodbye to various teachers who schooled them in the tried and true subjects of science, mathematics, literature, history, and many other topics of training to gird them, making them ready to succeed in society. The most important person in my life at that turning point became me. I knew Mom and Dad would always be there, but I had to take responsibility for myself. This became apparent as I struck out on my own.

Following two years of community college, I enrolled at a university. No one in my family had ever attended an institution of higher learning. I became the first. All during this time I was growing, learning about society, community, sexualities, cultures; in other words, the world around me.

By this time I knew what to call myself, a homosexual, or in more common terms, a gay person. I was attracted to men. Sometimes it was hard to miss seeing people like me on the news. Most always, stories about gays and lesbians had a negative slant. A common factor tied all the stories and news events together; the words, "They chose that lifestyle, so let it be so."

Lest you think like a lot of folk who believe I chose my sexual orientation, who believe I decided I liked men and it represented a purely sinful choice, such is not the case. Because of my close relationship with God – that is to say, as close as a humble follower can be – I prayed to God often, wondering why I was who I was.

Early on, I prayed. I prayed as a boy who could not understand why he could be someone whose very nature would disturb his parents. I prayed asking, "What is the reason for me being the way I am?" Sometimes nightmares filled my head as I thought about why would I want to even choose such a sexuality if my parents had such negative news of it?

As I came into my adulthood, my prayers wondered, "How could I be made into an instrument of peace?"

I was in my twenties when on Memorial Day weekend during an innocent shopping trip to a bigger town, I found all the stores had closed earlier than expected. What to do: go home and spend the evening with Mom and Dad watching television, or enter that gay bar in the downtown area I had heard about? Countless times around the block I went. What would I find inside if I went through those doors?

And then I found myself inside. It was an incredible place. Bright colors, loud music, and more people than I had ever expected.

So I was not alone after all. Others like me existed. These people did not appear sad or forlorn, nursing their drinks at a long, lifeless bar as the bartender looked on. No, these people were enjoying themselves, visiting, telling jokes, complimenting each other, offering to help each other out. In other words, a group of people at a favorite watering hole, just like any other.

By the end of the evening I was going home with a young guy I found very pleasant. And by the end of the summer I met a person whom I would deem my lover, someone whom I would love forever and move in with immediately.

Well, romance is fleeting and so neither of the relationships worked out. The guy I moved in with even proceeded to call me a hypocrite for having an intimate relationship with him and then going to church each Sunday.

Needless to say, loving coupling did not last more than several months after which I spent another few months extricating myself from the living arrangement.

When I looked back at my life, I felt I had to come to grips with my sexuality through my personal faith in God. I did not have a family that supported me. More often than not the people I met, although ethically fine, upstanding gentlemen and ladies, were not schooled in the Bible or in religion in general, possibly because they had been ostracized by the very people who should have exemplified love and kindness.

Often I had partners who did not even accept I was religious.

After all of the above, and now into what people who are my age would call their "senior years," I have tried to stay true to myself and to who I am. I admit I have probably not lived the best example of what a gay man should do in his life. I have made some bad decisions and I ask for forgiveness almost hourly. At the same time,

I constantly thank God for the riches He has given me. Richness of family, friends, and community, richness of a life lived well and full. I am eternally thankful for the love and joy and the promises He has given me. Such standards guide my life.

This peace stills my soul.

Today I live my life purposefully. I have a partner. We have been together a number of years. I thank God for him. I try to live as a Christ-like example to him and to all my friends. I trust that someday God will say, "Time for you to come home, son," and I will be with God forever.

God will ask if I have loved Him well and whether I have loved my neighbor as myself. I will answer, "Yes, I have earnestly tried to care for those who hurt, feed those who are hungry, and minister to those who are lonely."

Then I will take a deep breath and say, "I've had good and bad days. I've been a hypocrite and a liar. But I believe in You and trust in Your goodness and mercy."

I will hear God say, "I know." Then I will look forward to His words, "Well done, my good and faithful servant."

And I will enter into glory with God forever.

The author chooses to remain anonymous.

This is not something to be
ashamed of, but celebrated.

Brian Henning

Thirty Seconds Plus

by Brian Henning

My conflict with my sexuality began when I was in middle school in Pennsylvania. As a bigger kid who struggled with his weight and body image, I justified my thoughts and feelings as typical jealousy of my male classmates confident in their physiques. As I continued through high school and college, however, I began to realize my justification consisted of simply that – rationalization and avoidance. Yet, at the same time, I also got bullied through my school years for "acting gay." I came to believe I could not be gay, because then I would be proving the bullies right after so many years of denying it.

Once I began my seminary journey, I had a feeling I could no longer repress my identity. I cannot explain my awareness in words. I do know staying in the closet could not last as an option. After many sleepless nights, hours of reflection, and profuse prayers for clarity, I finally made the decision to come out to my family, friends, and colleagues. Every single person I told greeted my coming out with love and support. Joy and immense gratitude filled my senses.

Yet it also became clear the same love and support felt in coming out was not a universal response. I had heard the stories of hate and rejection toward others in the LGBTQ+ community, but that came from other places and from people whom we would stereotype as anti-LGBTQ+.

When I began the process for an internship site as part of my seminary journey, the potential supervisors with whom I interviewed met me with hesitation. Two congregations explicitly told me I would not be welcome in their community. I found opaqueness from the rest. Too often I received the response that, while most people would accept having an openly gay intern, some would oppose it vocally. Further, I often heard that the conversation was frankly too difficult to have so they avoided it altogether.

Not until a month after the internship assignments came out, however, did I feel the true complacency and discrimination of the Church. The church hierarchy informed me no internship site existed for me because the Contextual Education department could not find a congregation willing to welcome me into their community. I was crushed. I began questioning everything: my call, my identity, and even my belief in a loving, grace filled God.

By the love and support of my family, friends, and colleagues, I pushed on in my studies. I grieved, lamented, wrote our Presiding Bishop, and began talking. I talked to pastors, professors, and friends. I became aware of the deep, anti-Lutheran, anti-Reformation, anti-Gospel theology of scarcity and smugness throughout our church. But most importantly, I learned God had called me to be a voice in the wilderness – to challenge authority in our culture and proclaim the Gospel message of love and welcome for all.

I got rejected for an internship the same semester I learned about a theological concept called perichoresis. It holds one must be their true, authentic self in order to have a relationship with another. Specifically, we, as children of God, must act as our whole, God-created selves in order to live in a pure relationship with God and with others. What an utterly transformative thought. It helped me see the "box" which others had forced me into and stood inherently against the person God wants me to be.

Therefore, after even more conversation and prayer, I decided to take the next step in claiming my identity. I presently work as the Children's Ministry Coordinator for a congregation in Edina, MN called Shepherd of the Hills Lutheran. The staff and council president knew of my sexuality, but we never made a big statement about it. I never thought it relevant and so I never told anyone. Nonetheless, nondisclosure can become a part of living in the closet. I did not know how someone might react if I told them, or how the people they might tell would respond. So I said nothing.

After the events of the internship assignment process, though, I knew remaining in the closet in any sense of the idea could no longer serve as a viable option. So on Pentecost of 2017 at the end of worship, I told my story to everyone present in the sanctuary.

It was indeed terrifying, but also unbelievably freeing. I did not, however, expect the reaction. I figured some to be affirming, others to be vehemently against, and most to not really care. Instead, I received a thirty-second plus standing ovation. Not one person in the sanctuary remained seated.

After worship, the congregation further greeted me with hugs, kind words, concern for my well-being, and a sense of urgency to become a force and a voice of change. I felt awed.

Now I am well removed from the emotional pain of the above series of events. I am working on finding a new internship site for next year and am transforming into my new understanding of my calling. My ministry will not look like the traditional model of how people think of a pastor, and that is okay. In fact, it is a good thing. The church remains a unique place filled with unique people. This is not something to be ashamed of, but celebrated.

Some people who claim they are the church have hurt me. But they are not the church. The people who have restored me represent God's true church. I felt the love and grace of God through the love and grace of those who supported me. This epitomizes true faith and what God intends for us. God wants us to be whom God created us to be – special, extraordinary and in God's image.

God celebrates every aspect of our personhood. Anyone who claims discrimination justified by biblical interpretation needs to reread their Bible. God's story exemplifies deep, compassionate love for the children God created – all of them. Simply put, we are created in God's image and no one can ever take that away from us.

The church members who gave Brian the standing ovation offered him his internship experience and future call. He thrived at Shepherd of the Hills Lutheran Church in Edina, Minnesota from 2017-2021. Wanting to be nearer to family, Brian moved closer to home in 2021.

Shoulders

Yolanda Denson-Byers
(she/hers)

I have served as Senior Pastor of Shepherd of the Hills Lutheran Church of Edina, MN since July 2023. I am privileged to stand on the shoulders of Brian Henning, a deacon who 'came-out' while ministering to our congregation. I know if Brian had not taken such a risk, our church may not have had the courage to call me -- a queer senior pastor.

In my experience, when you act as your authentic self, you clear a path for those who need to follow. Brian's example made it possible for my congregation to dream of calling me. I stand on Brian's shoulders and I know others stand on mine. When I first became a pastor in the Evangelical Lutheran Church of America (ELCA), I did not know any other 'out' female, black, queer clergy in my denomination. Today I do. I am proud my wife and I have been so public about our love. Our example has encouraged others to do the same.

As a church leader, I teach that both pastors and lay people have a call to share the good news. We are all ministers. When we are baptized, we make the promise to "strive for justice and peace in all the earth." We are named, claimed, and sent out by the Holy

Spirit to fulfill our baptismal covenants. This binds us to justice work on behalf of those who experience oppression or marginalization, such as, racism, sexism, classism, and homophobia. We are called to welcome all people as Christ, to love unconditionally, and to see the face of God in every living being.

Our commitment to justice work means we can never choose silence in the face of victimization. In addition to leading lives of prayer and worshiping God in spirit and in truth, the Holy Spirit compels us to take a stand for righteousness. When we remain silent, victims suffer even more trauma.

We do not speak up only to change the mind of the wrongdoer, for we know we may – or may not – succeed.

We speak up so the injured know they are not alone. I have a friend victimized by childhood sexual abuse. People knew about it and said nothing. Their silence cruelly affected her, perhaps as much as the sexual abuse. It made her believe that there was no one on her side or she deserved the treatment that she got. For those within the LGBTQ community, whether someone on the outside speaks up against injustice represents a matter of life and death. People have killed themselves because they felt so hurt or so alone. Research has proven it only takes one person who is an advocate in the life of a young, queer, teenager, to serve as suicide prevention. Therefore, as persons of faith, we must speak up and speak out.

One way to make our voice heard is to vote our values. As tax-exempt entities, PFLAG (an organization for LGBTQ parents, family and friends) and churches may not legally promote political candidates. Instead, we are called to promote justice and to point out oppression. As Christians we believe in giving drink to the thirsty, food to the hungry, clothes to the naked, visiting the sick and imprisoned, and caring for widows and orphans. Our task, during the election cycle, is to hold up a mirror to candidates running for office and to vote only for those who have a proven track record of sharing the values of Jesus.

Genesis 1:26 reads, "So God created humans in God's image ... male and female God created them." As people of faith, we know all of God's children are beautifully created in the image and likeness of God - and we are very good! God teaches us deep appreciation for diversity through creation. Therefore, I choose not to hide who I am. I am loud and proud about being female, black, and queer and I cherish the privilege to feel safe enough to do so.

I have pledged my life to try to create safe spaces for others. In my own ministry, I do this via one-on-one's and small groups, as well as through my preaching, teaching, writing, and online ministries. Several years ago on Facebook, I created a Christian support group for LGBTQ young adults, 21-30 years old. We now have over three thousand followers from many different countries. In some of those countries, it is unsafe, even illegal, to openly be a part of the LGBT community. Our Facebook page represents one of the few places these people can glean information and support.

Sadly, so many people have been wounded due to their sexuality. Even in the church – perhaps especially so – adults and children have heard negative messages about themselves, in Bible study, confirmation classes, or even in Sunday worship. My wife says with the ring of truth, "There's no hurt like church hurt." As Christians, we must stop the violence. We must support those who have the courage to come out in our congregations, in addition to supporting the parents of kids who do so.

Our churches should stand as safe places to celebrate God's diverse creation. I have heard of churches who engage in naming rituals at the baptismal font when a transgender person reveals themselves and their new name to the community. What a beautiful practice in pursuit of justice and peace throughout all the earth. How wonderful would it be if the LGBTQ community ever came to believe in the allyship of Christian people?

I have a transgender child. You might think because I am queer, his coming out would have been easy. Not in the least. My first emotion was grief. I had dreams for my "little girl," with pigtails, to grow up to become a woman, wear a white wedding dress, and birth my grandbabies... That dream was not to be.

I had to do my own work, sometimes in counseling and always apart from my child, to grow into acceptance. Prayerfully, I put away my foolishness and supported the dreams of my child. I had to be teachable, sitting at his feet, and letting him tell me who he was. I learned my job is to love and support my child unconditionally. Parents think we have all the answers. But the Holy Spirit speaks to children as well. We must listen and learn. My son taught me our kids have their own journeys. We must follow the lead of our children and provide them with the resources they need to become their truest and most authentic selves.

Today I have the gift of a happy, healthy, holy, and whole adult son. He is doing great and he is alive and thriving. He did not kill himself as he struggled through his transition. He wasn't destroyed by the hatefulness of others – even by some in the church. Praise our God!

Parents, if your child is part of the LGBTQ community, especially if they are transgender, please believe me when I tell you there is something on the other side of your grief. You may be asking yourself, 'Will people look down on me? What will my family think? What will our church community do?' These questions are normal and natural. But I encourage you to ask another question, "What good can come out of this?"

For me, I grew into a deep relationship with my son, I made new friends, I found a church that supported us, and we grew closer as a family.

You are not alone. Please find organizations and support groups to accompany you. Find an open and affirming church. Introduce your child to happy and successful queer folks. Keep reading and take a look at the resources listed at the end of this book. As a parent of a black and transgender youth, my biggest fear was that someone would hurt him because he was different.

What I did not realize was that it was me – I was hurting him. When I decided to love my son unconditionally, it helped inoculate him against the hatefulness of others. When I taught him he was created in the image and likeness of Almighty God, it silenced the harsh voices of others. Finally, when I surrounded him – and myself – with a circle of loving people, we had a place of safety and security when we needed it most. I stand on Brian's shoulders, and now my son stands on mine.

I will say it again. You are not alone. An entire community of love, hope, compassion, and peace awaits you and your child. Be brave; step into your truth. I am a witness; the gift of your vulnerability will lead you into a new life – greater than you ever imagined. I am praying with you – joined by so many others. We have broad and strong shoulders, and we are upheld by Almighty God.

May God bless your sacred and holy journey into the newness of an authentic life in Christ Jesus. *May it be so.*

Rev. Dr. Yolanda Denson-Byers (she/hers) serves as senior pastor of Shepherd of the Hills Lutheran Church in Edina, Minnesota.

My only hope is that we
as a nation and as a people
can rid ourselves of
the hatred and bitterness
which has engorged us.

Carri Hoagland

I Feel Like a Woman

by Carri Hoagland

2018 ORIGINAL ESSAY

Mine has been an interesting journey to say the least. I was born in Texas, the Lone Star state, as Clifford Eric Hoagland. I was baptized Presbyterian and attended Sunday school and church. I did not have much choice since my mother served as organist. I remember sitting in the front row with a coloring book, subjected to my mother's scorn if I or my sisters did anything wrong.

After moving from Texas to Port Wing, Wisconsin when I was in middle school, my parents took me to the Lutheran church to attend Sunday school.

I remember my teacher and how we read the King James Version. None of it made sense. Of course my involuntary attendance didn't help matters. Memorization was important, even if we did not understand what the words meant.

Confirmation was pretty much the same. We had to do it, so all of us went. Since all my friends also attended, the group spirit helped us get through the entire ordeal.

After confirmation, church became the last thing on my mind. I was a young buck, carefree, and life was good. I never went to church except for a funeral or wedding.

In my early thirties I met the most wonderful and beautiful girl in the world. She grew up attending church, so we continued the tradition. We had three daughters, all of whom were baptized. Pastor Joe presided at two of our daughters' weddings on the shore of Lake Superior. We went to young couples gatherings and retreats and I became more interested in the way of the Lord and how God affected our lives. I realized the church leaned conservative, but at the time, it did not make much difference to me. Our children enjoyed Sunday school, vacation Bible school and other church activities.

Eventually a number of folks left the church because of infighting. My family also left. A couple friends attended a very conservative church a little distance away and we started going there. The Covenant Church had a large couples group. We remained very active. I helped in the construction of an addition because of the growing attendance.

As things went along, my life was going through monumental changes. After a lot of therapy, I began to comprehend I was transgendered. I also was retiring after twenty years of teaching at a technical college.

Because of my gender change, my wife and I separated. It certainly put a lot on my plate. My wife and I still love each other, not romantically or sexually, but as very good friends. We have three daughters and we saw no need to be hateful and bitter. My wife could not envision a relationship with a female.

While undergoing the change, my wife and I asked to speak to the pastor of our church. I should have known what might happen. I remember he had preached open hatred and denial against LGBT people.

We met one afternoon and told him of my major transformation. He never questioned or asked anything, but opened up the Bible to Deuteronomy 22:5 which basically says, "Men shall not wear women's clothes and women shall not wear men's clothes."

He closed the book and said I would not be accepted in the church. (He also told my wife later if I did appear, then he would have the ushers take me out.) As we left the church that afternoon while walking to the car, I crackled to my wife, "So much for the children's song 'Jesus Loves Me This I Know.'"

Needless to say, I never went back to the church and neither did my wife, even after we separated.

As things became tougher and more stressful, I needed to worship and be with the Lord. All my gender changes were going on during the last few months of my employment prior to retiring. One of the financial people at the college where I taught was a good friend and openly gay. Peter was one of the few folks with whom I secretly opened up, and he said, "Why don't you come to my church?" He said it was open and affirming. At the time I did not know what that meant, but I thought about it a little and one Sunday I went. I was still living a dual life, teaching as a male chauvinist pig during the week, and then on Sunday mornings sneaking out of my small town as a female. Talk about a nerve-wracking life.

I showed up and sat in the back pew near the door with an escape plan. Get up, left turn, out the door, and I would be free. I sat there. A nice elderly lady later known to me as Gertrude Jacobson, put her hand on my shoulder and said, "We are so glad you came."

That made all the difference. I started attending and eventually became an official member. I have done everything imaginable. I have cooked, presided over Bible studies, led the women's retreat, served on all the committees possible, sat on the director's board, and now I am teaching Sunday school. I was totally accepted at a time when I needed it the most, the time during my transition. The church is my family.

The women of the church threw me a shower prior to my trip to Thailand for sexual reassignment surgery. It meant the world to me. They traveled with me to the airport to see me off. Most memorably, my friend Tiss had the music changed at the Duluth airport as we walked in at 5:30 in the morning. It went from nice, quiet tunes to Shania Twain singing, *I Feel Like a Woman*. Tiss just giggled.

All of it was wonderful, but more importantly, I learned a whole different level of acceptance and love for God. No longer was I told what I had to believe. No longer was I told what I had to do to please my Higher Power. I did not have to fear God any longer. I got to understand God as I understood God.

God is the one who stands beside me and guides me. God reprimands me and then encourages me. I am not a perfect Christian by any means. I use four letter words. I have bad thoughts. I do things which I realize later I should not have said or thought about in such a way.

I now live knowing I will make mistakes, but with God's help I can correct them and make apologies. God stands now as my loving friend with whom I can have a quiet talk. God does not condemn me. God does not scare me. Sometimes I don't like what I am led to do because of the difficulty. I wonder where it all will lead.

I will end this chapter with perhaps my favorite memory. I recall waking up in the ICU from my surgery in Thailand. I am not one who has ever had a divine vision, for goodness sakes. But that night I remember looking down a foggy road not knowing what was at the end or how I would traverse it. Suddenly the road went on forever with no fog under a clear, blue sky. There stood a person in a white robe holding my hand. Not a word was said and I never looked at him, or her. It still brings tears even as I write this. I now know as long as I bring the Lord with me, anything is possible.

I think of a statement in our church. "We are pilgrims on a journey together seeking God's will on earth through study, discernment, and service. Amen."

Amen.

2024 ESSAY

Yes, I am getting older. I was born in 1943. But I don't let that bother me or let it serve as a marker of who I am. As a matter of fact, "Carri" only turned twenty years old January 7, 2024. My reassignment surgery took place in Thailand January 7, 2004. Wow, what an awakening after seven hours of surgery, coming out of anesthesia, hoses and tubes, half-way around the world, all by myself.

My first thought was, "What the he** am I doing?" The nurses were absolutely wonderful, even if they spoke almost no English. The care surpassed any I have ever had in this country. Ever since my surgery, the experience I had (when I first opened my eyes and tried to figure out what had occurred) has never left me.

I talked about it in my first story and I have got to tell you, it remains so vivid for me.

I opened my eyes and looked down a road. It was cloudy, foggy, and the road did not go very far. I could not see a thing. Suddenly, the picture changed. The road was straight, clear, a blue sky ahead. The road went on forever and someone held my hand.

The person holding my hand (she or he) was dressed in a robe. I did not look at their face.

I have used the memory of that image every day. If I have the Lord with me, then there are no boundaries. I share my experience at meetings I manage every week when talking about a "Power greater than myself." Life has been good. My only hope is that we as a nation and as a people can rid ourselves of the hatred and bitterness which has engorged us. We need to live as Jesus said, "Love one another no matter what."

Carri Hoagland, retired auto mechanics instructor, pilot and parent, is active at Pilgrim United Church of Christ in Duluth, Minnesota. She traveled around the United States giving talks on transgender issues for many years and continues to be a support for anyone who needs a compassionate, listening ear.

Acceptance

by Anonymous

I call my father a fundamentalist, evangelical atheist. My partner's father was a fundamentalist, evangelical Lutheran. Each was sincere and earnest in his position on existence, confident of his research into the basis of what he held to be true. Each thought his position stood as the only possible one. Those who did not agree needed to be convinced to change, converted.

In 1991, when I let my parents know my interests lay in men and not women, my mother was not completely pleased but very accepting. I think she wanted me to have kids. My macho father from whom I expected the worst commented, "Well, you're still the same Yann, aren't you?" What more could anyone want from anyone else on that subject?

To this day I get tears in my eyes when I think of my father's comment. Years later, after my father had met my partner and long before marriage became legal, he commented to me one morning, "If you were married, Adam would be my son-in-law." Again, I get tears in my eyes just thinking of that remark. It stands as one of the most accepting moments I've ever had on coming out. My father had completely accepted Adam as my partner.

My partner's rather large family consists mostly of fundamentalist, evangelical Christians of various denominations. His father once took my hand, stared into my eyes, and asked if I had taken Jesus as my personal savior. A few members of my partner's family (mostly, but not only, the younger set) have completely accepted and honored our relationship. Many others in the family have been very unaccepting. The outward displays of hostility toward my partner and me, mostly me, have stopped, but I suspect the internal sympathies remain not very different from where they stood at the beginning. I believe if I vanished from my partner's life, a great relief would settle among many in his family.

I had let my father know Adam was devout, comfortable, and happy in his Lutheran beliefs and asked him to lay off the conversion attempts. He did.

From what I know of Christianity, Jesus welcomed, honored, accepted everyone. Not so for most 'Christians' I have met. I always wonder what goes through the minds of each congregation member as the pastor preaches acceptance of people regardless of their skin color, their sexual orientation, their gender, their financial position, or any of the myriad aspects of humanity. Are they listening? Is their brain going 'not me' as she speaks? Are they busy reviewing their Netflix choices for the evening? They care greatly if they perceive disrespect of their religion on TV, in movies, in speeches, in print, but they do not seem to understand the relationship between religious doctrine and their life as they live it.

It is ironic to me that my atheist father was more able to find it within himself to accept a relationship between his son and another man than his Christian counterpart, my partner's father.

Acceptance

In 2018, due to fear for my safety, I have chosen to remain anonymous. In the USA, MY country as much as it is anyone's, because of the person I love, my financial and physical safety are in jeopardy outside certain areas of large cities. In September, 2017, in an amicus brief to my Supreme Court, the attorney general of my country advocated that businesses and governmental organizations be free to deny services to people who love someone of the same gender. How such people might be identified, stereotypes notwithstanding, is not immediately obvious. Something like the yellow stars used by Nazi Germany during the Second World War to identify Jewish people comes to mind.

The Divine Spark

When you are born
in a world you don't fit in;
it's because you were born
to help create a new one.

Anonymous

Odyssey to Kindness

by Stephanie Winter

Try as I might, I have always felt like an outsider and a nonconformist, although I've managed to appear as if I fit into mainstream culture. When the above quote floated across my Facebook feed, I realized in my own small way, it's always been up to me, a small town, sixty-two-year-old lesbian/feminist/chronically ill woman who has spent so much of her life longing for and working for acceptance, to provide a space for others to feel welcomed, cared about, and embraced for whoever they are in their deepest, essential selves.

 Yes, I am an idealist, a spiritual seeker, a philosopher and adventurer, an introvert, and a highly sensitive person. But labels only give you a sense of who I am; they do not reveal the inner workings of my soul. And so, I set out at a young age to begin my journey of a lifetime.

 My spiritual search – for the core of who I am – began on the farm where I was raised and continued when my small, southeastern Minnesota United Methodist church confirmed me. I was devoted to my church in a way the rest of my family was not. It provided friends, a community of support, and the opportunity to serve in the choir and as a Sunday school teacher. Every bit of it helped me feel good about myself.

In late high school I attended another church with my then boyfriend. We met in a congregant's home to listen to tapes translating the Bible directly from Greek and Hebrew. There I felt studious, serious, and special. By college, though, I broke away from the church to find something more meaningful and to explore my identity intellectually, spiritually, emotionally, and sexually. I could no longer rely on someone else to tell me what was sacred and how I fit into the larger universe. I needed to find out for myself.

My father and I could not know a letter he wrote post-college as I prepared to move in with a college boyfriend would direct the rest of my life. Both my parents expressed concerns about my decision to live with a man to whom I was not married. Although a sexual revolution had begun in the 1960s, cohabitation still served as the exception, not the norm. My father felt I had succumbed to peer pressure. In his letter Dad urged me to "march to the beat of a different drummer." From Henry David Thoreau's Walden:

> If a man does not keep pace with his companions, perhaps it is because he hears a different drummer. Let him step to the music which he hears, however measured or far away.

Neither Dad nor I understood the way he and Mom raised me and the unique person he encouraged me to become, in combination with the letter he wrote, would help move me even further outside societal norms. In 1981 I fell in love with a woman and embraced my identity as a lesbian. It had become clear to me, even though I had been in intimate relationships with several men, my strongest and most meaningful relationships had occurred with women. Nevertheless, I tried valiantly to fit into the confined circle of small town norms and motherly expectations: to become, first and foremost, a wife and mother. Consequently, after I reached my mid-20s and was living on my own in the Twin Cities, I also was reluctant and terrified to confront and reframe the expectations of everyone I knew, including myself.

By the late 1970s I had been volunteering for several years at Amazon, a lesbian/feminist bookstore in Minneapolis. Lesbian co-workers surrounded me and we catered to lesbian shoppers on a regular basis. My world and my reality gradually shifted and expanded. What became normal to me, however, had not become the norm for the small community of my childhood and adolescence.

I told my mother first.

Her response, "Don't ever tell your father. It will kill him."

I waited several years to write my dad a letter. As it turned out, my father, who at some earlier point had paid a short visit to Amazon bookstore with two of his older feminist sisters, was less surprised and less disappointed.

Several years later a medical diagnosis of Type 1, insulin-dependent diabetes shocked me. The world I knew shattered. My body was broken, my self-concept wounded, and my ability to be loved was destroyed. At least, that's what I thought. I felt incredible shame about my now imperfect body.

At age twenty-nine I was supposed to be healthy and vibrant. I felt alone and undesirable; thankfully, I found that wasn't the case. I will be the first to admit, however, maintaining a relationship while managing a chronic health condition has its challenges.

In the thirty-some years since my coming out as a lesbian and a person with diabetes, I can 'pass,' no problem. I don't look butch. I think I appear more androgynous. Also, you cannot 'see' my diabetes; unless you're around me when I pull out my blood testing machine or fill my insulin syringe for my early morning and pre-meal shots. I do not have the same struggles as some of my peers – gay men, butch women, and transgender people, whose appearance may not adhere to conventional norms and expectations.

I feel fairly comfortable in my own skin. Yet I occasionally find myself consciously or unconsciously evaluating how I will be accepted when I change jobs or neighborhoods, join new groups, or even sit down in my assigned seat on an airplane. I keep coming out to others over and over again about my sexuality and the diabetes, while I struggle to engage and prevail in the battle within myself for self-esteem and deservingness.

Regrettably, the human tendency to compare myself to those with more money, attractiveness, and intellect, and with better diabetes management (i.e., lower readings on their HbA1c tests) leaves me lacking. I am discovering my self-criticism only abates when I choose to accept myself and embrace my skills and abilities in addition to my flaws and failings.

Throughout my lifetime of seeking – my years of learning to live with, accept, and flourish – my identity as a lesbian and a woman with a chronic illness have influenced me more than anything. I have experienced how unhelpful it is to get judged because of my sexual preference or my physical inabilities. As a result, I have learned to open my heart and have practiced becoming less judgmental of the wide variety of differences between people of all races, cultures, sexual preferences, and abilities. I have learned the oft-forgotten truth that we are all One. I have chosen to walk upon the earth in a way modeled by my father, a farmer who revered beauty and silence, respected animals, plants, and all living creatures, and appreciated the never-ending cycles of life, death, and regeneration.

My lifetime journey has introduced me to a world of ideas

and other cultures through travels in Canada, Western Europe, Scandinavia, Mexico, and Central America, as well as other states in the U.S. In my early thirties I enrolled in a 'design-it-yourself' human development graduate program to discover how to live with chronic illness by balancing mind/body/spirit/emotions. While studying human development, I attended workshops and classes on empowerment, forgiveness, attitudinal healing, and psychosynthesis. I learned Reiki, a form of energy healing; the Chinese martial art t'ai chi ch'uan; and then t'ai chi chih™, a form of moving meditation, which I also taught. These have all had a huge influence on me.

Over the years I have meditated, prayed, read the Bible, attended spiritual retreats, gone solo on my own spiritual retreats, and explored shamanism and paganism. I have searched for – and found – people, words, images, and personal experiences which have fed me emotionally, intellectually, and spiritually. Some of the most important words came from Rachel Naomi Remen, a psychologist/writer/teacher/healer who wrote, "The purpose of life is to grow in wisdom and to learn to love better." To me, that represents a huge, magnificent, and worthy goal.

In 2002 after eight years together, my lesbian partner and I moved to live in the woods north of Bayfield, Wisconsin. It was glorious for both of us to revisit the peace and tranquility of living close to the land, under the trees, and within the web of existence. She also grew up on a farm. Our 'family' now included black bear and wolves, in addition to our geese, cat, and dog. Since we both were introverts, we could not have been happier.

The sound of the wind through the leaves, the song of birds, the stamp of deer hooves, and the long nights of silence blessed us. Of course, our relationship status preceded us. A man from whom we bought firewood told us he had heard two gay guys had bought the property where we lived. We did occasionally receive subtle and not so subtle messages about our lifestyle. Word travels fast in a small town. We worked hard to find connections and gain acceptance as we built a small health and wellness business.

Since transplants from Minneapolis–St. Paul, Madison, and other cities fill northwestern Wisconsin, we connected with former metropolitan residents who shared our values and experiences. We ourselves had lived thirty plus years in the Twin Cities. The old timers, people who had grown up locally and who had chosen to raise their families here, reminded us of our younger lives spent on the farm and the benefits of small town community life. Here we lived in the best of both worlds.

Unfortunately, the stress and pressures of dealing with my declining health, property upkeep, and different values and priorities split apart our partnership. We ended our almost twenty year relationship.

Now a resident of Washburn, Wisconsin, I feel as if I have become an accepted and valued part of the community. As I've grown older, I feel less of a need to explain myself or to live according to other people's expectations. Also, as my memories fade and I gain more self-acceptance, the pain of existing as an outlier in a society and culture that pressures and cajoles us to act, dress, speak, and believe in a particular way lacks the significance it once held.

In her memoir *Marrow: A Love Story*, author Elizabeth Lesser writes about her sister's dying process and their joint effort to heal their relationship:

> *...our own journey never ends. There is no finish line. There is always more to uncover, more to know, more to heal, more to love, more to give. Being true to oneself is a rough-and-tumble ride, full of challenges and wonders.*

I am on a lifelong odyssey. It asks me to become the most loving, accepting person I possibly can by welcoming and embracing those who struggle for love and acceptance, which, truth be told, is all of us. My spiritual search and personal experiences have taught me well. I can always be kinder. I can always aim to create more peace within myself. I can always open my heart just a tiny bit wider.

Steph Winter lives near Lake Superior where she walks its shoreline, breathes in lake air, and practices Spring Forest Qigong. She is blessed with friends who understand her need for quiet and solitude.

Surround yourself with a community that
will support and love you for who you are.

Jason Clifton

Will You Love the You You Hide?

by Rev. Jason Clifton

It was a crisp, sunny, October afternoon in Seattle. A year earlier at the age of 23 I sold my house, a half mile down the road from my parents' home. I packed all my belongings and moved 1700 miles away to Issaquah, Washington for school. I had lived in a small town my entire life. I was excited and terrified at the same time. Little did I know I would discover what it meant to be a beloved child of God, just as I was.

That October afternoon in 2007 I was at my practicum site as part of my service learning for college credit. I volunteered at an after school program. It was close to Halloween and a couple kids wanted to paint the nails of the adults. All of us obliged. On the way home I looked at my hands and realized who I was, my whole self. It dawned on me how much I had been trying to exist as someone I was not. "I was gay."

I am not sure what about that specific act and moment brought so much clarity. But then we don't get to choose those moments.

So began the process of coming out. A process as terrifying as moving across the country, only this time I was preparing to go it alone. Several friends I met in Seattle had been disowned by their families, fired from their jobs, and abandoned by friends and the church. We felt the structures upon which we relied to build our individual and collective identities had collapsed. Those calamities shaped my expectations of what I also would experience.

Having been raised in the Evangelical Lutheran Church of America (ELCA), I was attending a small liberal arts Lutheran college. I went to college with plans to attend seminary to become a pastor. But because of my self-revelation and subsequent coming out, I figured becoming a pastor would never happen.

My experience, however, had a different aspect than others. My closest friends from high school stood by me. An interim pastor, whom I had met only twice yet trusted because my mother trusted her, helped me come out to my parents. My brother and parents felt no surprise. My church community continued to support me. Make no mistake, I had to part ways with some friends, and the relationship with my sister remains a work in progress.

Nonetheless, even though my own coming out met with kindness instead of scorn, I knew the church could do better. We can teach the church how to exercise compassion and how to offer assistance. Many of us know what it means to hide one's identity from our friends and family. We found safety in hiding the truth, even from ourselves, as well as from God.

In 2009 the ELCA voted to ordain LGBTQ ministers who were publicly out and were in relationships. A pastor friend called and said, "Well, now you can go to seminary." So I did. I went to seminary and came to know other LGBTQ clergy and seminary students through Proclaim, a ministry of Extraordinary Lutheran Ministries.

What advice can I offer? Live into the person God has created you to be. Surround yourself with a community that will support and love you for who you are. Know there will be relationships which may end and others which take great amounts of effort. Most importantly, though, know you are a beloved child of God, just as you are.

You are a gift to the church. I close with my modified words from John Bell's song, "Will You Come and Follow Me?"

Love the you you hide.

Trust in God to quell the fear inside and never be the same.

Use the faith you've found to reshape the world around.

Jason Clifton has served as pastor at Our Savior's Lutheran Church, Solon Springs, Wisconsin since 2016. Among other ministries, their congregation has an active youth group and offers community book studies fostering discussions and healing in areas such as addiction, ableism, racial and native justice. Most recently they studied Austin Hartke's book, Transforming, the Bible and the Lives of Transgender Christians *and plan to read Brene Brown's* Braving the Wilderness *and Emmy Kegler's* One Coin Found.

Jason enjoys the outdoors, quilting, singing in choirs, attending area sporting events, and serving on the Solon Springs School Board.

Nevertheless,
the time has come
to share how much more
freedom we can realize
if we do not hide
what we do and
who we are.

Mark Ricker

I am an Episcopalian.
I am a Priest.
I am Gay.

by Rev. Mark Ricker

First, I cannot resist the need to apologize for those in the church who have, or who continue to judge you and tell you God does not love and accept you for who you are. Whether you are gay or straight, God made us that way and I celebrate you and hope you also find love and acceptance in the pages of this book and in the many and increasing groups and churches who also can give support. I welcome you and celebrate you too. God loves you and I hope to show you specific ways to see and understand that love.

Second, I want to let you know you are going to find, in growing numbers, that God is moving in our world and in our culture to allow more and more LGBTQ folks to experience the possibility of a more normal life, as well as ways to love whom you want to love without reproach or criticism. As with many other challenges in the life of the church and in our Western culture, it has taken a long time to accept mixed race marriages, to treat people of color the same way as white folks, to allow women the same rights and positions as men, and to advance other social justice and civil rights issues. Sadly, it often seems like the church takes longer than other institutions to find the way to love and accept when faced with such differences.

Furthermore, I hope anything of what I share will help you avoid some of the difficult things I encountered as a gay Christian in a world which did not accept both loving Jesus and loving others of my own gender. Thank God the scenario is changing.

When I attended high school one of my closest friends committed suicide because of some troubled spots in his life. Will and I belonged to a church which considered it a sin to be a sexually-active, exploring, gay teenager. People from our church, including me and his family, prayed God would deliver him from his 'condition' called homosexuality. God never answered those prayers. I cannot help but think those failed prayers pushed him to the despair which ended with the taking of his own life. The trauma of Will's suicide haunts me to this day.

At the time of Will's death, I decided I would never again participate in any activity that challenged how God made me, or how God made any friend or family member. Period. I had spent too much of my life living in the closet, but thanks to dear friends including others writing in this book, I have grown so much in my self-awareness and knowledge of God's Word, the Bible, and have been blessed to find new freedom in Christ. For some, however, my words may come as a surprise.

During my teen years and beyond, I was part of a very conservative Christian denomination. Rather than deal with my own gayness, I felt God wanted me to hide it, hence being in the closet proved to be a reality in my life. This led to stages of very low self-esteem and depression. I was told one could not be gay and serve Jesus. While I cannot say that I regret all of my related life choices during those many years, I can now promote a freedom in God in a healthier manner.

As a gay person growing up in a conservative Christian culture, I made many choices. Some choices we make in life cause us regret, and some do not. My choices enabled me to have a wonderful family and to experience things in my life which have helped me to become the person I am now. Nevertheless, the time has come to share how much more freedom we can realize if we do not hide what we do and who we are. If we remain in the shadows with internal conflicts and bouts of depression, then we cannot fully realize our creative blossoming in other areas of our lives. I now readily join in circles of friends who celebrate our sexuality. How wonderful it is to finally find such freedom in Christ.

I am encouraged by the 'Jesus Movement' which is happening in my denomination with an increased awareness of social justice problems. From LGBTQ rights to environmental issues, such as the danger of 'big oil' pipelines going through Native American lands and waterways, we are taking notice.

When North Carolina decided not to allow separate restrooms for transgender people, our new presiding bishop who leads our entire church, world-wide, sent a strong message to NC State Officials on June 10th, 2016. He let them know most Episcopalians did not like what their legislature and governor had done. Jesus rejoiced that day.

When authorities told Native Americans the pipeline in North Dakota would go through their water supply, my own Bishop from Eau Claire, Wisconsin went to serve alongside the protesters as an act of support and solidarity. Most Episcopalians supported his engagement. More and more, I see hope for the marginalized in our society. In fact, recently our presiding bishop issued a statement to the entire church. Michael Curry summarized:

> *When we are born anew through baptism, we promise to respect the dignity of every human being. Today, transgender people and indeed the entire LGBT community need us to keep that promise. By doing so, we can bear witness to the world that Jesus has shown us another way — the way of love.*
>
> – The Episcopal Church, Public Affairs Office, June 28th, 2016

Statistics show support for our movement. Teen suicide among LGBTQ teens is dropping now that marriage equality is the law of the land. This is good news. People feel more hopeful and included.

I help build shelters for LGBTQ young people in different areas of the U.S. In the past such shelters did not exist and gay kids had an even harder time having been thrown out of their 'Christian' homes. Homelessness devastates well enough, but when you are gay, the issues posed become even tougher. We endeavor to make their situation less traumatic.

I encourage you to watch the "It Gets Better" videos on YouTube. The message remains true. Life will get easier for you and for your LGBTQ friends.

The bullying that goes on in our schools, neighborhoods, and in society in general needs our attention more than ever. Appearance, gender-questioning, and the desire for young people to explore and understand their identity stand as essential issues to normal growing and healthy living.

The New Testament tells us Jesus came into our world to set us free. When we judge other people, Jesus tells us we are wrong. He came to set us free to be who we are and free to love all people. Unfortunately, humans still build walls, rather than welcome and celebrate others and their diversity. Much work remains to be done, but, thanks be to God, doors are flying open. Even church doors. The light of God's love and acceptance is gaining ground and is growing in power and good understanding. Bright lights are shining. More help is on the way. Extraordinary people from around the globe are speaking out, coming out, and sharing their new, convincing, and healthy understanding of human sexuality. God is at work. God's freedom will prevail. Love must prevail. The time has come.

I pray the age-old cycle of fear and hate will further subside and God's perfect love will cast out, perhaps force out, fear.

Mark has been an Episcopal Priest for more than ten years. He has pastored a number of churches in Wisconsin and Colorado. He is now retired from full-time church ministry and continues to work tirelessly to promote LGBTQ rights throughout the U.S. It is his hope that this book will bring encouragement to all who read its stories. Mark has served on the PFLAG Washburn board for several years.

The Divine Spark

It remained hidden, not allowed, and
therefore so much larger
within me.

Anonymous

McGregors Are Queers

by Anonymous

Someone chalked 'McGregors are Queers' on our driveway. I was 14. Summer of 1969. I can still feel the disgust of my father scuffing out the word 'queers' while he spat *do you know what that means?*

I knew full well what it meant. That word was me and I was being scuffed out. That part of me could never be. Never see the light of day. But THAT WAS indeed all there was of ME.

As a teenager, without my sexuality, little else existed. I could concentrate on nothing without my sexuality screaming at me. Raging hormones and budding awareness of sexual attraction are endemic to being a teenager. Having to hide sexual attraction is an almost insurmountable task. Sexuality permeates everything a teenager does and thinks, 24/7. But I, and everyone else, hated mine. It remained hidden, not allowed, and therefore so much larger within me.

When necessary, along with everyone else, I laughed and insulted people who seemed to fit my feelings so others wouldn't suspect me. And as I vilified others, I knew the scorn could easily be directed at me.

The Divine Spark

It's particularly insidious when what is hated isn't obvious. The people with power invited me to participate in hate for myself. For self-preservation, I did. At least if the hate were directed at short people or fat people or Native Americans or black people or people with Southern accents or Semitic people or people with an obvious difference, the subjects would not be expected to participate in the slander. The haters might actually wait until the hated were not within earshot to spew their vitriol.

The writer chooses to remain anonymous.
The surname "McGregor" is a pseudonym.

Freak Out to Peace Out

by Katie Makolondra

Life as a teenager in an ultra-conservative part of Wisconsin was the worst. To begin with, I had non-traditional parents. My mom had a physical disability and I viewed my dad as an elderly man because he was twenty years her senior. They were nonconformists and political philosophers. The one good thing was we attended the "hippie" church in town that housed a brilliant, liberal pastor who preached the values of being human. He did not spew any controlling, literal interpretations of the Bible. We had no fire and brimstone at Hope United Church of Christ, only good feelings and a strong, supportive community. Our church, however, was in the city of Sturgeon Bay, far from the boondocks of my school district's boundaries.

All my classmates were religious. This is not hyperbole. The kids in my class were either strict Catholics or the kind of Lutheran where men sit on one side of the aisle and the women on the other, all in silent reverie of the pastor's threats of eternal damnation. I did not fit in at all.

I recall my first experience at my best friend's church one Sunday morning. She warned me it would be boring, but made consolation promises of Schwann's ice cream sundaes afterward. The sermon

The Divine Spark

dwelled on David and Goliath and burning in Hell. Every time the pastor mentioned, almost casually, burning in Hell, he looked right at me. I have seldom felt as hated as I did that morning. It penetrated my heart. At that moment I convinced myself he knew I was weird. And by weird, I mean queer.

The slow realization I was a lesbian sunk in like molasses in winter. In first grade whenever Nora came near I had my first collection of butterflies fluttering in my stomach. She and I would play married couple, complete with kisses and cuddles. It seemed innocent enough to the outside, I am sure, but for me I knew our "friendship" wasn't normal.

At nine or ten years old, while watching a horror movie, I asked my mom if it were possible for me to have a crush on girls. I remember getting red in the face and a little sick to my stomach just asking such a shameful question. She laughed at me and assured me I liked boys and I definitely did not like girls that way. I begrudgingly accepted her opinion, but it didn't sit right. My attraction to beautiful women was strong.

As I got older I had crushes on all my best friends with increasing intensity. I became obsessed with Tiffany; simply had to have sleepovers at Jamie's house; and don't get me started on Julie.

Yet I knew enough to establish public crushes on boys to avoid becoming the target of a witch hunt. I always had an overarching sense that being gay out loud would endanger me. I would get bullied relentlessly and possibly attacked. Actual gay bashing truly existed where I came from and the idea of getting caught, then ostracized and injured, terrified me.

Nevertheless, one can hide the truth for only so long. In seventh grade, I developed the strongest feelings I had ever known. Actual love. Jodie stood out as a funky, oppositional rule-breaker.

She was not a girlie girl. She was crass, she smoked menthols, and she had a boy haircut. Jodie was perfect. After swimming at her cottage, I will never forget as we showered in our swimsuits to get the lake off our skin. I felt compelled to wash her hair. I desired intimacy and actually went for it without thinking.

As I started massaging shampoo into her hair, she looked at me – and 'looked' is not the right word. She knew me with her eyes. Her smile faded. She pushed me away and got out of the shower still full of shampoo.

Jodie had me call my mom to come pick me up. She stopped answering my phone calls and threw the notes I had passed to her in the trash. Worse yet, Jodie told people.

I had already served as a target for bullying because of my unusual, non-local family, and my individuality. I always prayed – literally prayed – nobody would figure me out. But now kids started teasing me, calling me dyke, laughing in my face… and this was the only interaction I received. Nobody wanted to have sleepovers. Nobody wanted to hang out. I was the loneliest I had ever been. My once-friend's mom called me a "fat dykey hoe" to my other friends at an awards ceremony.

No tears could fall fast enough from the amount of pain I suffered. I began cutting myself and started smoking. Eventually I fell into a group of misfits who self-medicated their quirks away.

Thankfully, my own church, my sanctuary away from the emotional suffering as a queer teenager, became the first church in our region to openly accept gay members. I remember the day like yesterday. The gay and lesbian congregation members put rainbow stickers on their name tags and we hung rainbow flags around the inner worship area. I swallowed everything and memorized the faces and names of the queer members of my church. These people always existed. I had never known they were LGBT. If I could have known sooner, I would have had an outlet for all the confusion and frustration. Maybe I could have shown more bravery. Yet, this one gesture by Hope Church actually gave me hope. I realized maybe someday I could live as openly gay. Could someday hurry up?

In high school my friend Amy, who knew nothing of my sexual orientation, took me in during hard times. She went to my church. I felt certain I could tell her my secret without repercussion. After a night of liquid courage, I asked her if I could tell her something. I was sick to my stomach from nerves, but felt confident she would be throwing rainbow confetti and celebrating my coming out. Wrong.

I told her I was "bi," not even true, but it felt safer than straight-up lesbian. Amy left the room. She would not let me sleep in her room anymore and preferred I find an entirely different living situation. My heart dropped to the floor. I couldn't stand the rejection. I felt betrayed by my own self. How could I have let my guard down? Didn't I know better than to trust anyone? Amy finally did come around, but our friendship had changed forever.

The accumulation of false starts and failures pushed me deep into the closet. I decided I would call my endless longing for female companionship a horrible fetish, if not a curse. I tried to ignore my nature. At college, I dated a few women, all disasters, and therefore sought a different type of relationship. I met my now ex-husband and hunkered down internally for a life of regret and sacrifice for the greater good of fitting into society.

We had three children, built a wonderful life together, and enjoyed a legitimate friendship. A friendship I could no longer keep as I got older.

I turned thirty and went to Minneapolis with my best friend for a night of dancing and cutting loose. We ended up at the Gay 90s, an awesome LGBT nightclub, where I locked eyes with a foxy, butch lesbian. We danced all night.

When I woke the next day I told my friend I was totally a lesbian. "What do I do? I have a husband. I have kids! Should I keep waiting it out until the baby is eighteen?" We strategized and planned.

I went home to a very honest and painful conversation with my husband. We began to detach emotionally from one another and started the process to end our marriage.

Without Messiah Lutheran I could never have legitimatized my identity as a lesbian. I joined the church to help ease my mind about the monotony and misery of marriage by focusing on the other joys of life and on God's ultimate plan. I am a firm believer in God and find solace in His ways, but I particularly needed the moral compass delivered by Pastor Nancy's sermons. Pastor Nancy accepted my struggles and guided me through the most difficult times. I thought my love for my husband served me well enough to carry me through life. He remained a dear, dear friend, but I felt no passion. The touch of a man made me feel violated. I was stuck and Pastor Nancy helped me come to accept the path laid out for me by God.

I was never an abomination, as my former community believed. I was a child of God. My place in His eyes did not change as a lesbian.

I am out and stay fairly vocal about it. I work in a middle school and want any other questioning students not to suffer as I did. I want to serve as an advocate and a mentor. Though the past remains dark and sad for me, the present and future look much better. I am so grateful to have faith and to receive support in my faith here in the north woods. No more suffering in the heartland.

Katie works as a Special Education teacher at Bayfield Public School, Bayfield, Wisconsin.

How can I reconcile the two?
My queer friends said,

You cannot.

My Christian friends said,

You cannot.

Michael Van Uytven

Divine Favor

by Michael Van Uytven

I remember very clearly when I first decided.

I was sitting in the woods by myself. I had fasted for a day and a half. I was in college and as part of my Outdoor Education Immersion semester we did solo camping experiences, alone, in the woods, for two days, without food in my case. There wasn't a soul around. I was reading Teddy Roosevelt's *The Man in the Arena* speech.

> *It is not the critic who counts: not the man who points out how the strong man stumbles or where the doer of deeds could have done better. The credit belongs to the man who is actually in the arena.*

For some time then I had struggled. Over a year to be exact. I struggled with being Christian and queer. How can I reconcile the two? My queer friends said, "You cannot." My Christian friends said, "You cannot." Both sides of my identity tugged me in opposite directions – I was torn, not entirely sure I would continue as a Christian. Yet, I decided to stay. Teddy Roosevelt's words made me realize something. If I leave the faith, then it gets worse for everyone. I was aware how easily one could give up and drop out of the church when the world is against you. I have no animosity for those who lost their faith because of conflicts with their church. But I decided, alone in the woods, I would walk a different path.

Another pivotal moment occurred the following winter. I took a class called theologies of liberation with Charlie Krysinski. I am forever indebted to that class for expanding my mind and showing me how I can follow my commitment to the oppressed through my commitment to Christ. The tenth Psalm says,

> *O LORD, you will hear the desire of the meek; you will strengthen their heart, you will incline your ear to do justice for the orphan and the oppressed, so that those from earth may strike terror no more.*
>
> Psalm 10:17-18

There, in that classroom, I began not only to hear the words of the Psalmist, but feel them in my soul. Two years have elapsed since then and my conviction remains steadfast.

As of this writing, I am reading *The Institutes of the Christian Religion*. The theologian, John Calvin, writes, faith,

> *is a firm and sure knowledge of the divine favor toward us, founded on the truth of a free promise in Christ, and revealed to our minds, and sealed on our hearts, by the Holy Spirit.*
>
> Institutes, Book 3 Chapter 2 p. 360

Without entirely realizing it, that type of faith always resided within me, and I never feel it stronger than in moments of righteous indignation.

I will never forget the day my friend told me she was not religious but she had talked to some Christians who told her God did not love her. She then said she didn't care because she's not Christian. She might not care but I fume. That conversation daily sears itself in my mind, because I do care. I do care that hatred and deceit have squashed the boundless love of God. I do care that the grace of Christ is abused everyday by those who despise me and my kin. I do care that those who profess Christ act depraved, wicked, vile; they act slanderously, greedily, and without love or mercy – in short – like the devil.

I have had a taste of divine favor and I will not let it go. James Baldwin writes,

> [W]e, with love, shall force our brothers to see themselves as they are, to cease fleeing from reality.
> *The Fire Next Time*, p. 10

I have had too much fill of the divine glory to cease from my path, compelling my brothers and sisters in Christ to see themselves as they are. I am convinced God loves me and regards me as their child. I demand to be treated as a child of God, as an heir to inestimable glory. I will keep making that demand until the day I die and pass unto everlasting glory,

> [f]or I am convinced that neither death, nor life, nor angels, nor rulers, nor things present, nor things to come, nor powers, nor height, nor depth, nor anything else in all creation, will be able to separate us from the love of Christ Jesus our Lord.
> NRSV, Romans 8:38-39

Michael graduated from Northland College with a bachelor's degree in Outdoor Education and a double minor in Philosophy and Religious Studies. He lives in Ashland, Wisconsin and hopes to get a master's degree in Divinity. He would like to take a leadership role in the church. He enjoys reading, lifting, biking, running, snowshoeing, martial arts, hanging out with friends, and attending the United Presbyterian Congregational Church.

Mom and Dad assured me
this was the best thing for Andrea;
this was what would make her
happiest in her life,
and that's what they wanted
for all their children.

ten-year-old Caroline

My Sister, My Brother

by Niki Pohnl

I am the proud parent of three children – Caden, 22; Anthony, 19; and Caroline, 12. My oldest son Caden came out to us as transgender three years ago. It affected each person in our family differently.

    I worried mightily about Caden's emotional and physical well-being during his coming out. I could not begin to understand what it was like to live his life. It got me thinking, what has it been like for his siblings? I know how I see the process, but what about Caroline, then nine years old? What has she noticed? Where has she seen change? What has she learned? Does she struggle? At times I saw my daughter reflect on how she once had a big sister, and I know she grieved that loss.

    I had to write a paper for a class I took last year. My task was to interview someone who went through a traumatic event and compare it to the five senses. I chose to interview my daughter Caroline, by then age ten, one year after the transition started. I hoped it might help her recognize how far she has come through the process, how much happier her older sibling became, and how to identify the support she has around her in anticipation of another traumatic experience in her life.

From Caroline's interview:

What is it like, being a sibling of a transgender person? I have an older sister and an older brother. If you had asked me a year ago about what it was like to be a nine-year-old with two teenage siblings, then I probably would have answered with heartfelt stories about family movie night, family game night, family meals, and times I got to hang with them in their rooms – a big deal to me. Asking me the same question at age 10 is a little different story, because now my big sister is transitioning to be another brother. Put yourself in my shoes and hear what my last year has been like.

In the beginning, transition felt very sad. So sad I would not have my sister anymore. I was used to having a brother and a sister, not two brothers. I didn't go to school for two days after I found out. I just wanted to hold my teddy bear and be close to my mom and dad. Transition felt confusing. Why would she want to do this? What else in my family was going to change? Why wasn't my mom crying about this like I was? Transition felt scary. How was she going to change? What would she look like? Will she still like to hang out with me? What if I make a mistake and call him 'Andrea?' Will she be mad at me? Or will he be mad at me? I asked my mom to take down some of the pictures of me and my sister because it was a reminder of who she wasn't going to be anymore.

At the same time, transition felt comforting. Mom and Dad assured me this was the best thing for Andrea; this was what would make her happiest in her life and that's what they wanted for all their children. Transition felt calming as we prayed for her every night. We prayed God would help her make the best decision for herself, and we prayed that God would keep her safe in the process. Transition felt reassuring as I talked to the school guidance counselor about grief and began to understand what was happening to me and my family.

Transition sounds mixed up. Sometimes I hear my sibling

referred to as Andrea and sometimes Caden. Sometimes I hear and say 'she' and sometimes I hear and say 'he.' Conversations sound so confusing. I hear us being so good about the change in name and pronouns, until we talk about the past and we refer to 'she' and 'Andrea,' and then our words get so mixed up again.

Transition also sounds like some friends and relatives refusing to make the name change.

Transition sounds like anger. The first few months of the testosterone shots, Caden was angry a lot. He got angry with me for leaving my dance bag on the living room floor. He got angry with me for not getting to bed exactly on time. 'No worries. It's not his problem,' Mom would say when it made me sad. Little things just made him angry.

Transition sounds like Mom saying the same thing over and over, 'We have to be patient. It's the drugs entering his system that make him this way right now. When his body gets used to the drugs he will be more pleasant to be around.'

Transition sounds like a funny voice change.

Over the past year, transition at my house looked like change. Caden's bedroom color changed from purple to white and different pictures went up on his walls. Caden's bathroom products changed. Pictures in our house began to change.

Transition looked like correction. Always correcting ourselves when we said 'she' or 'her' or 'Andrea' when we meant to say 'he,' 'his,' or 'Caden.' Actually, I am the best at the pronoun transition, more than anyone in my family.

Watching my brother transition looked like shots, drugs, and injections on a weekly basis. It looked like hairy legs, hairy armpits, and larger gauges in his ears. Transition looked like a binder, a dress shirt, and a necktie for work.

And transition smelled like Axe body wash.

Along the way, transition has felt like family support.

> *Watching us interact like the family we always have been no matter what we are going through – highs and lows at dinner time, bonfires in the back yard, openly talking about the process.*
>
> *Transition feels like school support. Mom and I talked to all of my teachers before 4th and 5th grades so they knew about our family dynamics and they knew how best to support me when I was at school.*
>
> *Transition felt like summer therapy. Learning about what it all means and watching the process unfold made the transition easier for me.*
>
> *Transition feels like comfort. Comfort in knowing this is what my brother wants and it makes him happy. Comfort in still getting to hang out with him once in a while, because I love that!*
>
> *Now, transition feels like love and acceptance. Transition looks normal. Saying 'he' is easy for me. And one of the proudest moments for me during this transition so far was that he changed his name to Caden so his name would start with the same letter as mine. I love my brother no matter what.*

It is my hope the parents of another child, or the sibling going through a similar situation, will recognize the resilient nature of children and how they grow to become accepting, non-judgmental, and well-rounded. People told my husband and me they felt sorry for Caroline having to go through something like this at such a young age. Yet we feel blessed. Caroline sees people as people and does not judge, question, or care about their gender. Caroline has learned what it is all about. It is all about love and respect.

> *Caden is now a school teacher in the School District of La Crosse, WI and working on his master's degree. Caden aspires to teach high school math. He lives in a healthy relationship with his partner.*

Love Conquers All

by Mary Bondeson

One of my favorite memories as a mom is my son coming out to me. He had been having a classmate come over after school, and it became obvious to me they wanted to be together. Yet, I was still surprised when he stood before me, shifting from one foot to the other, hands jammed into his jeans pockets and said, "Mom, I've been wanting to tell you something for awhile, I'm just gonna come out and say it: I'm bisexual!"

"Oh, I thought you were going to tell me you're gay!"

No less than four months earlier, I offered a familiar refrain that I often tucked into our heart-to-heart conversations about relationships and life plans: "You never know, you might be gay. And that would be ok."

He countered: "Mom, I'm pretty sure I'm not gay!"

Growing up, my son had free reign in our household to play with clothes, hair, persona, hero roles, heroine roles, you name it. I figured why shouldn't a boy have as much fun being as expressive as girls? His older sister took great delight in dressing him up in her now-too-small fancy clothes and jewelry. They had a treasure chest filled with colorful fabric, all manner of skirts and dresses, capes, high heels, masks, wands, fairy wings, hats, make-up. While my daughter had fun with perms and braiding hair, my son would use glitter glue to make outrageous mohawks in neon green or blue. A favorite memory is seeing him layer a dress over another dress, a skirt on his head which he swished this way and that as though he had long hair, several layers of bling around his neck, and high heels. Sword in hand, he would race up the slide bottom to top, then leap in one bound from the upper platform to the ground. He was a stealthy ninja flying around the yard in a fantasyland of his own creation; in other words, he was being a healthy fun-loving kid.

These escapades did not go unnoticed by others who were not as comfortable as I was with not labeling how my children played. A sister queried if it was "normal." My husband squirmed to find out his son wore a dress to a community dance. Our day care center prohibited him from wearing skirts or dresses "to make sure he didn't get teased." I never stewed over the relationship between creative play and sexual identity/orientation. We could hire researchers to study this, but really, who cares? I'm sure they would find that of the many children who engage in creative dress-up which blurs the gender "line" (it's not really a line, but that's another issue), some are gay, some are bi, some are trans, some are straight, and some don't care to designate!

Negotiating situations that came with his first boyfriend presented some difficult challenges. His friend was not ready to come out to his parents, knowing that their strong Christian upbringing was at odds with his sexual orientation. We had many conversations about privacy, secrecy, and confidentiality. I took an oath not to "out" them to anyone, knowing that in a small community, if my friends knew my son was gay, that news would soon spread. I felt robbed of a rite of passage enjoyed by every mother of a teenager: sharing the joy of your child's first romance. Instead of excited phone calls, facebook posts, and fun chats during soccer games, I was counseling two boys to be careful to never get caught holding hands in public, much less share a kiss.

I had always welcomed into my home everyone whom my children cared about. If they were friends and they behaved in respectful ways, they were part of our family. Our place became the safe place for my son's gay friends. As many of them came to know me, they would confide some of their personal struggles and family conflicts. It was painful to know that many of these teenagers did not have unconditional acceptance at home. Revealing their sexual orientation came with the risk of being rejected, or not having a place to live. Their uncertainty and self-doubt created a very palpable vulnerability.

This story has a happy ending, however. Or, more accurately, my son's life continues to unfold in happy, healthy ways. Within two years of coming out to me, he forgot I was still living under the vow of secrecy: "Mom, I've been out at school for a long time now!" His school administrators protected and supported him. His first boyfriend finally gave his parents the ultimatum after his first year at college: either you stop trying to convert me or I won't be coming home any longer. They did.

My son knows himself. He digs deep to uncover his own truths. He is compassionate, caring, articulate, interested in life, adventurous, excited to learn and grow.

In preparing this story I asked my son to share his thoughts. The following statements are paraphrased.

> My parents were liberal and I knew they were progressive in their views about gays; I had gay family members who were loved and included. Still, it was an act of courage for me to come out. It doesn't make sense. It's not logical to say I knew it would be okay AND it was difficult to do, but it was. I was nervous and anxious. Maybe because I had experiences as a kid where I was shut down for how I expressed myself. It took me several years to come to terms with my sexuality. As early as six years old I was curious about being with both girls and boys.

> I knew this was not the norm. I felt like it was wrong even though it was natural for me.
>
> I carried this internal conflict all through my coming-of-age years. I pushed this away for a long time. Not until I had the experience of being with a boy and being intimate did I know if this was right for me. Likewise, I needed to explore being with girls to eventually understand that although I appreciated girls, my so-called attraction was more a desperate attempt to lessen the burden of my true identity; to make it seem I had some aspect of normalcy, like I was half normal instead of being straight up gay.
>
> Homosexuality in our society is stereotyped as just a sexual issue. But it's so much more than that. It is intimacy, connecting with another human being, sharing yourself, being included socially, doing fun things together, introducing new people and new things to each other. Regardless of your sexual orientation, there remains a fascinating mystery of who you choose to partner with.

Let's keep fighting to protect every person's right to love whom they choose to love.

For those who struggle with accepting the gender revolution that seems to be sweeping our world, I would offer some tidbits to encourage open-mindedness:

1) **Educate yourself.**

   Read people's stories, find out about new language used to describe gender identity and orientation. Explore resources. Some of my favorite websites are:

   www.glsen.org

   Gay Lesbian Straight Education Network is a powerhouse of information regarding teen issues surrounding all forms of sexual identity and orientation, with comprehensive resources for schools, teachers, and students.

www.pflag.org
> *Parents and Friends of Lesbians and Gays* also includes transgender people and the rainbow of expressions and orientations that are blossoming in our culture right now. Find a local chapter near you and attend meetings. There is no substitute for face-to-face dialogue and you will meet some of the nicest, most caring people on the planet.

www.gendercool.com
> This user-friendly site supports transgender kids and gives a healthy and positive face to the label *trans*. Their resource pages alone could turn someone's life around, whether you are trans yourself or you are an ally. It is upbeat, up-to-date, and filled with helpful information.

2) **Start talking.**

   Speak with friends, family, and community. Ask questions. Listen. Withhold judgement. Mull over new ideas. Ask more questions. Turn to love. Repeat.

3) **Let nothing interfere with your love.**

   Jesus and the Beatles were right.

The evening my son came out to me was followed by a long, full talk about his new boyfriend and how he was going to negotiate situations with school, friends, and family. He took charge by insisting on controlling his coming-out process. He considered how his news would affect different family members and made thoughtful choices about how to introduce (or not introduce) his new boyfriend. He was fifteen. The joy I felt that he would share this with me was so great I immediately popped to my feet and gave him a huge, teary-eyed hug. After several hours of conversation he said, "Mom, could we possibly not talk about this for, like, at least two weeks?"

I don't have a gay son. I have a loving, caring, compassionate, intelligent, engaging, and thoughtful son who happens to be gay. I couldn't be more proud.

Mary Bondeson lived in Washburn, Wisconsin for 34 years with her two children and husband John Mydels, where they founded and ran the Friends of the Earth Garden Center and the Harmony School of Music. Mary now lives in Indianapolis where she and two of her sisters care for their elderly mother.

Fathom

Truly knowing another person remains one of the great mysteries of life. To feel the deep movements of joy and grief, to have an authentic connection, allows us to transcend time and space and enter a sacred moment. We are built for connection with each other. The sense of separation, aloneness – division if you will - harms not only our individual health, but the health of our communities and our society. When we support and value each other, we experience a sense of fulfillment that enriches our lives.

Our United States Declaration of Independence enshrined the human value that all have the right to pursue happiness. Merriam Webster defines happiness as a state of well-being and contentment. As a therapist for more than forty years, I believe happiness includes an inner sense of contented wholeness. Happiness runs far deeper than the passing happiness we experience when we eat something delicious, see a smile on a loved one's face, or get a long hoped for gift. That kind of happiness comes and goes with external circumstances. Deep well-being and wholeness comes from having a sense of congruence, integrity, and acceptance – most especially self-acceptance.

What makes one person happy often baffles another. Truly knowing and deeply understanding the inner experience of another human being, even when they try to tell us in their most articulate way, remains one of the greatest challenges of the human condition.

The Divine Spark

The difficulty of understanding what makes another person tick – to gain a sense of their inner experience – takes a great deal of work. The inability or refusal to gain such an understanding can lead to all kinds of conflicts in families, between friends, and in our society.

Every person has many experiences unfathomable to anyone else. I once had such an experience with a very close friend of mine. Rae had suffered a major stroke. I visited her only a couple days after it happened, early in her hospital stay. Nurses would come and go, showing her pictures and asking her to describe what she saw. They held the picture in front of her, just at the distance one would hold a book. She described in detail everything on the right side of the picture, and nothing on the left.

Rae was paralyzed on her left side. She had no use of her left arm, hand, leg, or foot. She could not turn over. She could not get out of bed. But it was more than that. If I stood on her left side and talked to her, she remained vague, hardly paying any attention to me. If I moved to her right side, we could have a conversation. At one point I said to her, "Rae, you're going to have to find the left side of your body in order to get well." Rae was several years older, and always very dedicated to her health. If Rae needed to find the left side of her body, then Rae would start now and work until she did.

Rae lay in bed. She then raised her right arm in the air and waved it around. I could not understand; to fathom someone waving their right arm around in front of them trying to find their left side. Rae had absolutely no idea where the left side of her body was. I could barely comprehend.

About three months later, Rae moved into a nursing home, undoubtedly for a long-term stay. She called me one day very angry, not only at me, but at her daughter and her doctors. Rae said, "No one told me I was paralyzed!"

I was stunned. How could she not know she was paralyzed? Not only had Rae lost the use of her body and the sensations of her body, she had lost all awareness of the left side of her body. Rae did not know it existed and had absolutely no sense there was a problem with it. The peculiar state of Rae's consciousness represented something I simply could not fathom. If you have a left side of your body, then how can you not know it exists?

Something similar happens as we age. I am now in my late 60's. I feel very young, more like a young 30-year-old than a "senior" citizen. I look in the mirror and think, "Well, what happened there? You've got wrinkles!" I want to climb up a ladder and clean the gutters, but my body says, not so fast. My sense of myself does not match my body. In my youth I remember looking at "old" people assuming they must think and feel as their bodies look. I remember my surprise when my grandmother at age ninety-seven told me, "I feel like a little girl inside."

Our brains process information coming from our senses and from our bodies based on specific neural circuitry. Rae's brain had completely lost contact with the entire left side of her body and thus did not even know it existed. We possess a sense of ourselves not necessarily tied to our bodies, such as when older folks feel young.

We often assume everyone understands the world and experiences life the same way we do. What we perceive and believe, we assume, must be what everyone else perceives and believes. After all, we live in a world of common denominators. Unfortunately, when we expect people to experience the world the same way we do, and then someone else has a very different experience, our world becomes disorienting. Cognitive dissonance, an uncomfortable inner state, can occur when we expect one thing with such certainty that upon encountering something different, we simply cannot wrap our heads around it.

As parents we often fear for our children when they make choices we perceive as unwise. Sometimes the facts support our fears. When we, as parents, however, expect and ask our child to abandon a fundamental inner knowing, and then to live according to our assumed facts about them and about life, we are asking them to abandon themselves for our sake. When a gap lies between one person's truth and the subsequent expectations of others to behave accordingly, then that gap creates room for unhappiness, distress, and psychological symptoms. The greater the gap, the worse the symptoms. When we demand someone live by our standards and values rather than their own, we create a gap between us and them. Feel those words, us and them. The gap between us and them fosters fear, hate, misunderstanding. How painful. We fall victim to our desire to be right. We hurt ourselves and we hurt others. We miss a deep, rich opportunity for connection and love. We miss a chance to instill hope and offer blessing.

Most people have their identity grounded in their bodies. Who are you? I am a woman. I am white. I am 5'5" tall. This is such a profound assumption that we accept it as basic reality. My friend Rae had no awareness of the left side of her body. If what and who she was at that point was exactly the same as her body, then she would have been only half herself. But Rae was still fully Rae. Rae did not know of her paralysis – something I could not make any sense of until she told me. It lay beyond my comprehension.

For most of us, comprehending that someone could have a male body, yet possess a profound sense of femaleness makes no sense, let alone trying to understand it. How can you have a male body and feel female? If our sense of gender perfectly matches how our bodies are shaped, then we assume our sense of gender must come from having our particular body. If I had been born with a male body, then most certainly I would feel male, right?

Not necessarily.

Most of us think of sex and gender as synonymous. In fact our biological gender may be very different from our gender identity. Gender identity represents one's own inner sense of gender. People do not make a conscious choice about gender. I have always had the feeling I was female. I did not make a choice about it. I could move to Canada, become a citizen, and change my national identity to Canadian. Nonetheless, I could not make a choice to feel inside that I am a man. Transgender folks do not make a choice about their sense of gender as different from the biological characteristics they possessed at birth.

An additional factor may influence gender identity. The animating force within all humans has a gendered aspect. Such an idea comes from a purely personal experience. When I was pregnant with my youngest daughter, I felt certain she was a girl. I felt so certain that when the sonogram showed male genitalia, I was deeply confused. I proceeded to raise a boy with all the gendered cultural expectations that go along with bringing up a young man. When she told me she was in fact a girl, some part of me was not surprised. Some part of me had known all along. It still took a lot to get used to the idea. I had conditioned my mind that I had a son. Changing pronouns and names was, and sometimes still is, challenging.

The difference between an inner sense of gender and a body with incongruent sex characteristics creates a gap. The gap for transgender people can cause extreme distress. When we do not understand and appreciate the gap, yet another gap arises - the distance between us and the transgender person. If we know of the incongruency and disagree with the person's "choice," the second gap widens even more and increases the trans person's distress.

We cannot ever fully understand another's inner experience. The best we can do, the most compassionate, loving, honest, honorable, respectful thing we can do lies in trusting the inner sense another human has of themselves. We can offer the grace and permission, both as individuals and as a society, to allow people we may not understand the right to pursue a sense of wholeness and well-being, the pursuit of happiness, that most basic human right. It will enrich ourselves to give permission to risk accepting, welcoming, and learning to know those who are different.

When my daughter first began to reveal to me that her gender identity was different from the one assigned at birth, I felt as if she were finally living fully connected inside her own skin. There was a subtle but palpable difference in my sense of her as a human being.

After my daughter had her gender affirming surgery, I could see a profound change in her. I could see happiness behind her eyes for the first time. A calm settled deep inside her. I had never realized her disturbed inner peace. But now, the pain she had experienced in her transition was replaced by a profound sense of joy and well-being.

And although I have worried about her because of those in our society who endanger trans folks' lives, I feel a deep sense of elation at her happiness.

For my daughter, hiding her sense of herself cost her something. I grieve not fully knowing her when she was younger. My daughter hid her gender for any number of reasons. The gift I now have of truly knowing her remains a most precious treasure of my life. My sense of connection with her, the privilege of walking with her through her transition, being her mother, I would not trade for anything.

If our society simply accepted others who are different from us as the beautiful gifts of the Divine that they are, then we would not need Pride parades; the so-called transgender "agenda" would not exist. There would simply be people living their lives, pursuing happiness and well-being. They already exist as our children, parents, siblings, friends, and neighbors. LGBTQ+ folks would love to be able to live their whole selves with you in the easiest, natural way possible. Our society's resistance to their ability to live fully cheats them, but also cheats us of the joy of truly knowing those in our families and communities. Closing our hearts and closing off avenues for others to pursue life, liberty, and happiness harms not only them – and it most emphatically does harm – it also harms us. Opening our hearts blesses those who are different from us. Moreso, our open hearts bless us.

Jeanne Clark is a mother of two daughters and a psychotherapist living in Northwest Wisconsin.

Eat. Work. Play. Vote. Love.
Forever and always.

Kate Stolp

Mama Bear

by **Kate Stolp**

Conceiving a child and giving birth unleashed an animal instinct I did not know I had. I am a Mama Bear – and you don't get between a Mama Bear and her cubs.

I have two sons. One is gay. One is bisexual. I am often asked: "What is 'that' like?" My answer is: "The most precious and unparalleled experience I have ever had." The stages go kind of like this:

Sleep. Cry. Eat. Poop. Sleep.

Sleep. Eat. P oop. Walk. Talk. Play. Sleep.

Sleep. Eat. Play. School. Play hockey. Sleep.

Sleep. Eat more. School. Play hockey. Play tricks on Mom. Sleep late.

Sleep. Eat more. Grow facial hair. "Mom? I need to tell you something. I'm gay."

Mom replies: "Is this another trick?" and quickly realizing it's not, says: "I love you. Have a nice day at school."

Just like that.

Yep, that's exactly how my gay son's 'coming out' happened. My bisexual son came out during a phone call home from college: "Hi Mom. Stuff at school is going well. Having some fun. Also, need to tell you that I am bisexual." Me: "How does that work?" He explained his love is not linked to gender. I learned. I loved him. He has such a big heart.

I was surprised both times. Why surprised? My son's coming out occurred twenty years ago. The visibility of today's LGBTQ+ community did not exist then, so untold numbers of people were "covering." Those were scary times.

The path outside the 'closet,' while still dangerous, held many pitfalls. My kids have to walk that path. But the biggest reason for the surprise lay in my "heteronormative" self. I did not realize with all the "Sleep. Eat. Poop. Play" stuff going on, in the deep recesses of my mind, I had a dream for my childrens' futures which involved marrying someone of the opposite sex.

My great hope resided in protecting my precious ones from all the bad things the world can bring. In that 'Coming Out Moment,' I realized my dream would not happen. My children would walk a difficult road, at risk of verbal and physical harm, ostracism, and even death. I grieved the loss of my dream and feared for them.

The grieving did not last long, because frankly, nothing had changed. Though it would be difficult, I knew that if they chose to, they could find someone to love and to love them back. They would be okay. My dream simply looks a little different now.

My fear for them deepened as I learned more about their rights, or lack thereof. Fortunately, especially for people in their age groups, the rest of us are so much more accepting today.

Unfortunately, my sons do not have equal rights in the United States of America. Many people threaten my childrens' abilities to thrive in our society. My children risk discrimination at work and school, in financial and legal systems, housing, and the job market. Because of our laws and attitudes in Wisconsin, my children do not feel safe in this state, and I doubt they will ever return. My children have been bullied, suffered as the butt of off-color jokes, and feared they would lose their jobs *if someone finds out*. Worse, too many people believe that my sons cannot love whomever they want. Too bad for Wisconsin – they are intelligent, well-educated, talented, sensitive, honest, amazing, loving people.

I am very proud of my sons. My heart aches for their pain. I strive to protect them.

I need your help. We need our senators and representatives to understand how love works and to vote in favor of the Equality Act so we can protect all our children.

Eat. Work. Play. Vote. Love. Forever and always.

Kate Stolp retired as a Mayo Clinic physical medicine and rehabilitation physician. Currently she works part-time at the Red Cliff Clinic, Red Cliff, Wisconsin. In her free time she is active with the Chequamegon Democrats, volunteers for PFLAG Washburn, volunteers as a master naturalist, and loves to ballroom dance. She and her husband live in the Chequamegon Bay area.

There is no longer Jew or Greek,
there is no longer slave or free,
there is no longer male and female,
for all of you are one in Christ Jesus.

Galatians 3:28

Grace Upon Grace

by Rev. Dale Chesley

I was raised a Lutheran; but more in the tradition which defined a Christian by what I did not do, than how I lived through Christ. A Christian doesn't smoke, drink alcohol, do drugs, take God's name in vain, or have sex outside of marriage; a few among the plethora of 'don'ts.' The same Lutheran tradition viewed the Bible as a sacred book that gave us a mandatory and absolute guide for our lives. If a person wanted "salvation," then one received Jesus as Lord and Savior and followed the rules. As a result, faith became something which demanded my responsibility, and God stood as the One to whom I remained responsible.

Such standards about right and wrong loomed large. I had to live the right life and avoid all sins which brought judgment upon me. Sexual sins sat at the top of every list. Dealing with my own sexuality ate at my conscience, and when the church taught me the abomination of homosexuality, it came as a relief in certain ways because I was not homosexual. At least I got that one right. I sinned elsewhere, plenty, but the one about not becoming a homosexual came easy. I did not understand homosexuality and had little incentive to try, because here we had one sin I did not struggle with. I learned homosexuality represented a sin, a Biblical standard, no arguing about it.

Another Biblical standard taught me to reject the idea women could serve as pastors. The tradition of our church had no room for it because the Bible taught it was wrong. But as part of the American Lutheran Church, we eventually voted to ordain women, and that confused me. Nevertheless, I remained faithful to my teachings.

When I attended seminary, the sins initially taught to me were challenged in a number of ways. It made me look at women in ministry differently. I also learned new things about what the Bible says.

I remember back in my confirmation classes a surprising word caught my attention. In Luther's meaning of the second commandment, "You shall not take the name of the Lord your God in vain." Luther tells us to not use God's name superstitiously. How might one do that? The best I could come up with was the ways in which we used God's name like a good luck charm. For example, if a person crosses themselves before shooting a free throw in a basketball game, thinking God would then help them make the basket, that felt a bit superstitious to me. Superstitions almost always have their roots in fear. As I studied at seminary, I started to see how often I looked at the Bible superstitiously, out of fear, instead of love.

In 1 Timothy we read these words:

> *Let a woman learn in silence with full submission. I permit no woman to teach or to have authority over a man; she is to keep silent. For Adam was formed first, then Eve; and Adam was not deceived, but the woman was deceived and became a transgressor. Yet she will be saved through childbearing, provided they continue in faith and love and holiness, with modesty. - 1 Timothy 2: 11-15 NRSV*

That kind of settled the issue of ordaining women as pastors.

But it also ignored completely Galatians 3:28:

There is no longer Jew or Greek, there is no longer slave or free, there is no longer male and female, for all of you are one in Christ Jesus.

Suddenly I realized the faith I grew up with had no good way of dealing with contradictions in the Bible. In fact, it denied any contradictions existed. The word 'superstitious' took on a new meaning. If we bring to the Bible confessions of believing it presents one unified understanding of God without cultural influence, then we approach Scripture with a closed mind rather than an open heart.

When in seminary, I met three women in my formulation of faith group. I watched them. I listened to them. I witnessed the embodiment of Galatians 3:28. Obviously the women differed from me physically, but in intellect, in sense of call, in gifts for ministry, in love for Christ, in sense of humor, in passion for the Gospel, I saw no differences aside from our individuality. I recognized some would make better pastors than I would. It was not my place to deny the work of God in them.

Besides, I have never believed for a second that women would be saved through childbearing. I have always believed they would be saved the same way I am saved, through the grace of God, because of the cross and the resurrection of Jesus Christ.

In spite of some superstitious discomfort from my old way of understanding things, I found myself joyfully and confidently embracing the decision of our National Church to ordain women.

Change often comes slowly. Even though I began to believe our church should ordain women, I continued to believe homosexuality amounted to sin and disqualified such people from ordained ministry. But an example had been set and I believe the Spirit of God was at work in me.

I don't know if Tony Campolo was the first to say it, but he said Jesus would never say, "Love the sinner, hate the sin." I have heard many people say the same about gay people. On the other hand, he also suggested Jesus would say, "Love the sinner, hate your own sin." I ask myself, what does it mean to hate my own sin? I have come to believe it means I don't have time to focus on the sins of others. I have all I can handle to hate my own sin. I had to ask how such a view would guide me in my understanding of homosexuality from a believer's standpoint.

Again, I had to look at Scripture and question whether I had rooted my search in superstition. Romans 1 contains text about men and women who stick their fist in the face of God by denying their natural sexuality in order to seek sexual relations with members of the same sex. Such a passage does not describe a young teenager struggling with his or her desire for a person of the same sex. They are not rebelling against God. They simply realize they are wired differently and are trying to cope with what it means in a society filled with so much condemnation, a society which hates others' sins.

As I have listened to the voices of homosexuals, I hear them saying they made no choice in the matter. It is the way they are born and they are living out what is natural for them. Then I hear heterosexual people claim it is a choice. Yet it makes most sense to listen to those who live through the experience, rather than claiming to defend an ideal which often originates from their own decision on how to interpret the Bible.

As I have tried to figure out what I believe, given my history, the Bible remains at the vital center of my convictions. Time after time, as I ask what Jesus might say about homosexuality, a scripture comes to mind. Since Jesus says nothing about it, we need to listen to other things he said. I had no desire to change my mind about homosexuality simply because it became the current trend in society.

The scripture Matthew 21:28-32 kept occurring to me. Speaking to religious leaders Jesus says, "What do you think? A man had two sons; he went to the first and said, 'Son, go and work in the vineyard today.' He answered, 'I will not;' but later he changed his mind and went. The father went to the second and said the same; and he answered, 'I go, sir'; but he did not go. Which of the two did the will of his father?" They said, "The first." Jesus said to them, "Truly I tell you, the tax collectors and the prostitutes are going into the kingdom of God ahead of you. For John the Baptist came to you in the way of righteousness and you did not believe him, but the tax collectors and the prostitutes believe him; and even after you saw it, you did not change your minds and believe him."

Jesus said the people the religious leaders considered sinners, people on the fringes of society, would go into the kingdom ahead of them. From a young age this has greatly offended me. I could not understand the message from Jesus because I considered myself one of the religious ones. As I have come to understand the ways of Jesus, it makes sense. He always has a heart for those whom everyone else would condemn.

When I asked the question of who comprises those people today, given the context of the opinion of many religious leaders today, I understood homosexual people fall into the category of those fringe people. Many church people today, who hate other peoples' sin rather than their own, point fingers, exclude, and draw the circle of grace in such a way as to leave gay people out.

I have come to believe Jesus wants me to love the ones on the fringe in the same way; to recognize they go into the kingdom of God ahead of me should I point my finger at them, instead of hating my own sin. I have become cognizant anytime I draw the circle of grace in such a way that if it leaves anyone out, Jesus will stand outside the circle with them.

It is clear to me being homosexual does not constitute a sin. It is also clear to me I am guilty of all sorts of actions I believe are sinful. I have to focus on my own sins for which I seek the grace of God. Likewise for homosexual people. If God does not condemn their committed, loving relationships, then I will stay out of it. I have enough to worry about with my own sin.

In some ways I remain captive to the superstitious ways of my past which I must deal with all the time. I now acknowledge I possess no qualifications to name other people's sins. I can see the Bible does not speak with as much clarity concerning homosexuality as some would claim. God has moved my heart to yield to God's love. I have gay friends who lack nothing in spiritual gifts compared to straight friends. I have gay pastor friends who have proved themselves effective, loving spiritual leaders in Christ's Church. They are called in the same way I am called. They live as redeemed sinners, no differently than my life as a redeemed sinner. God makes use of them in the same ways God makes use of me.

I sit today with open arms to those who are gay and also want to do ministry. I see them as whole people in the faith since all of us remain broken in some way.

It is not an easy thing to examine how hate and love find their place in the life of the Church. I hold the opinion the righteous cannot rise to the level of "hating the sin but loving the sinner," as many would have it. But I also believe the sincerity of the sentiment and those who say such things often speak from the center of their hearts. They seek faithfulness to God and to what they believe God wants. Yet I also believe many remain captive to a superstitious way of understanding the Bible and thus find it impossible to consider God might call to God's flock someone they believe the Bible labels sinful. I say this not to justify such actions, but to observe more love emanates from them than often gets received. Loving, faithful people whose self-righteousness means they shun homosexual people have hearts which want good things for gay people. They strive for faithfulness to God, but like all of us, they live as saints and sinners at the same time.

Nonetheless, such heartfelt convictions still hurt gay people, the hatred admittedly scathing at times. Hatred in the name of love is still hatred, a great failing of the church I love. I confess it as our sin.

For me, the example of Jesus loving those on the fringes compels me to do likewise. I invite them, in Jesus's name, to the center of the circle of grace. I am one also invited and Jesus is the host. Our circle stands as a place of holy fellowship. I welcome as I have been welcomed. Christ loves all of us, together, and we offer that love back in the way we care for his body; in the way we care for each other.

Married with two grown daughters, Dale served as pastor at Good Shepherd Lutheran Church in Ashland, Wisconsin until his retirement in 2019. However, forty-one years of full-time ministry was not quite enough for Dale. He still loves serving as pastor in an interim capacity.

The Divine Spark

The term "evangelical" comes
from the Greek word euangelion,
meaning "the good news"
or the "gospel."

The good news of Jesus
is good news for everyone,
and *everyone* includes all
beloved LGBTQ people.

The word evangelical is also used
to describe those who fight
against the rights of LGBTQ people.
Choose instead to be a joyous, radically
inclusive evangelical.

God's Justice, God's Love

by Rev. Nate Aaseng

Those who believe the Bible condemns same-sex relationships subscribe to a Sacred Writ view of biblical authority. Sacred Writ believes the Bible itself represents something close to divine, that it says exactly what God wants it to say, and nothing more, in exactly the words God wanted it said.

If you truly believe such a point of view, however, then you cannot pick and choose which parts of the Bible you accept and don't accept. If you believe God condemns homosexuality because of selected verses, then you also must believe it an abomination to:

- eat pork; Leviticus 11:7-8
- eat shrimp, clams, oysters, scallops, crab, lobster, and squid; Leviticus 11:10-12
- do any work on the Sabbath, under penalty of death; Exodus 35:2
- let your furnace run on the Sabbath, even when it's -20 degrees outside; Exodus 35:3
- wear any clothing made of blended material; Deuteronomy 22:11

- shave or trim your beard or have a tattoo; Leviticus 19:27-28
- be a woman and wear pants. Deuteronomy 22:5

Furthermore, if you believe God condemns homosexuality in the Bible because of selected verses, then you must believe these with equal conviction:

- More than simply condoning slavery, God says beating a slave to death comprises righteous behavior so long as the slave survives a day or two. Exodus 21:20-21
- Polygamy violates no law of God – the patriarch Jacob had four wives.
- God not only tolerates genocide but sometimes demands it. Joshua 8:24-27, 10:40
- A defiant child must be stoned to death. Deuteronomy 21:18-21
- God requires you to sell all you have and give the money to the poor – you do not have a choice. Luke 18:18-22
- No one who is lame or has a visible defect can become a pastor and no one who has a blemish can approach the altar for communion. Leviticus 21:18-21
- It is shameful for a woman to read a lesson or say a prayer in church. I Corinthians 14:34-35
- Acceptable behavior includes offering your daughters to a mob to be gang raped. Genesis 19:8

When people complain that denominations such as the Evangelical Lutheran Church of America (ELCA) is no longer a Bible-based church, they mean the ELCA is not a Sacred Writ church. It never has been. ELCA follows the teachings of Martin Luther, who urged people to read the Bible in light of its central claims of who God is and how God relates to people.

If one reads the Bible in light of the central claims of what God embodies and how God relates to people, the Bible tells a very different story than what critics believe.

Look at biblical texts central to faith from a law perspective:

1) In Exodus 20 we find the Ten Commandments. The issue of same-gender relationships does not appear.
2) In Matthew 22:36-40 Jesus is asked to name the essence of the law. He answers, "Love God and your neighbor." Again, homosexuality has nothing to do with it.
3) Galatians 5:14 contains a similar essence of the law. Homosexuality remains a non-factor.
4) Jesus never spoke one word about homosexuality.

Given all the above, as a matter of Jesus's commands, a Christian cannot consider committed, same-gender relationships as central to the message of the Bible.

On the other hand, Exodus 22:21-24 holds high the issue of justice for the poor, the oppressed, and the stranger. This focus occurs so often in the Bible one must consider it a principal message.

In Luke 16:19-31 failure to do justice amounts to the only sin that got the rich man sent to hell. Again, the meaning of the story remains clear — justice rides paramount.

In Matthew 25: 31-46 injustice encompasses the sin that sends people into damnation.

In Matthew 18: 23-35 someone owes the equivalent of hundreds of billions of dollars. God forgives it all. God forgives everything in this story except injustice.

The Bible states over and over that God always stands on the side of the oppressed, the downtrodden, the powerless. Given the extremely high suicide rate of LGBTQ youth and their exposure to relentless ridicule, hatred, and discrimination, who gets more oppressed than they?

How do we determine whether same-sex relationships present as a law issue (though the Bible says not an important one), or as a justice issue?

For guidance, we can rely only on our experience with God's creation. If, in one's experience, those in committed, same-gender relationships actively recruit, corrupt, and threaten the stability of the family and culture, then we face a law issue.

If, in one's experience, they are simply people who happen to be wired differently, then we face a non-issue.

If, in one's experience, they occupy a place as good friends or family, you share their pain and heartache, and feel for the abuse and persecution they experience physically and emotionally, then we confront a justice issue.

Given what the Bible says about God's absolute hatred of injustice, given Jesus's disgust with the Pharisees harping on their morality laws all the time, the Bible states unequivocally, if we should err in this matter, we had better err on the side of justice.

Pastor Nate Aaseng served as lead pastor at St. John's Lutheran Church in Eau Claire, Wisconsin until his retirement in 2019. Before pastoring, Nate worked as a research microbiologist and free-lance author of 178 published books. After retiring, Nate continues to write and recently published a new book, I Wonder: Mind-Freeing Encounters With God.

The Next Step

by Aubrey Thonvold

As we honor the holiness of each person named and claimed by the Divine, it is important not to stop there. Love lasts as a powerful emotion which can transform many lives. The work of welcome, inclusion, and celebration of lesbian, gay, bisexual, transgender, queer, intersex, and asexual (LGBTQIA+) people continues throughout life, manifested through advocacy.

Faith communities have a number of options on how they can live a lifelong journey of supporting LGBTQIA+ people. ReconcilingWorks, a national non-profit organization, is committed to accompanying people and ministry settings through outreach, education, and support.

Ministries across the USA and Canada have an opportunity to partner with ReconcilingWorks to join a national coalition of Reconciling in Christ (RIC) communities. This coalition consists of synods, congregations, seminaries, campus ministries, and Bible camp ministries who have approved a public welcome statement of all sexual orientations and gender identities. These congregations live out their welcome in unique and evolving ways to meet the needs of their communities and the people they serve. Their work endures as life giving and life saving for LGBTQIA+ people. The power of being named, seen, and cared for can transform lives. To read such welcome statements, watch video vignettes of the diversity of congregations, and to learn more about the resources available, please visit www.reconcilingworks.org.

Working side by side for justice and equity for others, we can reclaim the power of scripture. We can use it to bring healing, wholeness, and liberation for a community of people historically told they count for less based upon stagnant scriptural interpretation and manipulation of authority.

For those who are LGBTQIA+, live boldly in the truth you are fearfully and wonderfully made. Without you living as the beloved person you are, this world would not survive. As a queer person myself, I need you to show up and walk alongside me so I can live as my best self, knowing I remain whole, valued, and loved.

For those of you who join as allies, ask members of the LGBTQIA+ community what we need from you. Trust us to know what works best for ourselves.

If you define yourself as someone living with questions, then continue to seek understanding and remain open to what you may learn and receive.

We can only accomplish our holy work when we are in relationship to the Divine and to one another. May our hearts and minds stay open to performing beyond the "Golden Rule" of "treating others as you want others to treat you." Let us aim for the "Platinum Rule" of "treating others as they would want to be treated."

Aubrey Thonvold is the Executive Director of ReconcilingWorks, based in St. Paul, Minnesota. The publisher of the first edition of this book, Messiah Lutheran Church, Washburn, Wisconsin, is a Reconciling in Christ (RIC) congregation.

Resources

WEBSITES

FaithfulAmerica.org
GenderCool.com
GenderSpectrum.org
glaad.org
mhawisconsin.org/prism
pflag.org
TheTrevorProject.org
TransmissionMinistry.com

Here are a few good reads recommended by *The Divine Spark* authors:

Raising Kids Beyond the Binary: Celebrating God's Transgender and Gender-Diverse Children
by Jamie Bruesehoff, Foreword by Sarah McBride

Tomorrow Will Be Different: Love, Loss, and The Fight for Trans Equality
by Sarah McBride

The Lavender Scare: Gay and Lesbian Life in Post WWII America
by David K. Johnson

A Brief Guide to Ministry with LGBTQIA Youth
by Cody J. Sanders

Queer Virtue: What LGBTQ People Know About Life and Love and How It Can Revitalize Christianity
by Rev. Elizabeth M. Edman

Queer Clergy: A History of Gay and Lesbian Ministry in American Protestantism
by R. W. Holmen

Transforming: The Bible & Lives of Transgender Christians
by Austin Hartke, updated in 2023

Wrestling with God and Men: Homosexuality and the Jewish Tradition
by Steven Greenburg

You Gotta Be You, How To Embrace This Messy Life and Step Into Who You Really Are
by Brandon Kyle Goodman

PEOPLE

Go to **pflag.org** to find PFLAG groups everywhere.

Go to **pflagwashburn.org** to find ways to connect with other like-minded people in Wisconsin's Chequamegon Bay area.

Go to **reconcilingworks.org** to find LGBTQ friendly churches nationally, and ELCA churches in the Chequamegon Bay area of Wisconsin, including Bethesda Lutheran Church in Bayfield, Immanuel Lutheran Church in Cornucopia, and Messiah Lutheran Church in Washburn.

EMERGENCY MENTAL HEALTH

All help is provided with confidentiality.

877-565-8860 Trans Lifeline

866-488-7386 The Trevor Lifeline
Trained counselors are available 24/7 for those who are in crisis or anyone in need of a safe and judgment-free place to talk.

800-273-8255 Lifeline
Your call goes to the nearest crisis center in the Lifeline national network.

National Suicide Hotline
Dial **988** for help by phone, or text the word **HOME** to 741741 to exchange messages with a crisis counselor.

RELIGIOUS RESOURCES

The following are listed (starting on the next page) among the many religious resources found on National PFLAG's website:

https://pflag.org/resource/pflag-national-faith-resources/

There you will find MANY resources from a wide range of religious traditions; Christian, Muslim, Jewish, and interfaith/non-denominational groups, and also non-Judeo-Christian/Abrahamic denominations such as Unitarian Universalist and Buddhist, which reinforces how many faiths embrace all people, regardless of sexual orientation and gender identity.

Affirmation

Affirmation is an organization for LGBT Mormons, their families and allies. They strive to provide a safe space where gay Mormons can ask questions, find answers, and connect with others who have gone through similar experiences. They also hope to help people reconcile their sexual orientation/gender identity with their spiritual and cultural heritage as a Mormon.

The Association of Welcoming and Affirming Baptists: The Association of Welcoming and Affirming Baptists is the only organization devoted to supporting LGBT Baptists and their allies in the United States. They strive to support churches, organizations, and individuals who are committed to the full inclusion of LGBT Baptists in church life and mission.

Believe Out Loud Video: How to Be Welcoming

This great four-minute video from Believe Out Loud shows some of the basic steps that Christian faith leaders can take to become a welcome and affirming congregation. It includes information and best practices for anyone interested in learning more about ways to make their church more inclusive.

Brave Commons: Seeks to elevate the voices of LGBTQ+ students working within and beyond Christian universities in the United States.

Canyon Walker Connections

Canyon Walker Connections is maintained by Kathy Baldock, a straight evangelical Christian who has dedicated her life to improving the relationship between faith communities and the LGBT community. Kathy has also organized a social media project called Str8 Apology, is available for speaking engagements, and maintains an extensive list of resources for LGBT Christians and their allies.

Catholics for Equality

Catholics for Equality was founded in 2010 to support, educate, and mobilize Catholics in the advancement of freedom and equality at the federal, state, and local levels for LGBT family, parish and community members.

Dignity USA

Dignity USA is a chapter-based nonprofit organization founded in 1973 to serve LGBT Catholics and their allies. They stress the need to provide safe space where LGBT Catholics and their allies can share personal and spiritual concerns, participate in the sacramental life of the Church, and focus on education and social justice issues.

Fortunate Families

Fortunate Families ministers primarily with Catholic parents of lesbian, gay, bisexual and transgender daughters and sons—but welcomes families of all faiths. When parents explore and value their personal stories, they are empowered to share that story with their family circle, their faith community and the larger society.

Fellowship of Reconciling Pentecostals International

The Fellowship of Reconciling Pentecostals International is a network of Pentecostal ministers, churches, and ministries which seeks to reconcile all repentant people to God through the full gospel of Jesus Christ, without regard to race, gender, political persuasion, economic or educational status, sexual orientation, nationality, religious affiliation, or any other thing that divides.

FreedHearts

A Christian organization supporting LGBTQ and their families deal with family, religious and community wounds. Fee-based courses offered in addition to support groups.

Integrity USA

Integrity is a nonprofit organization of LGBT Episcopalians and their straight friends. Integrity has been the leading grassroots voice for the full inclusion of LGBT persons in the Episcopal Church and their equal access to its rites. However, advocacy is only one facet of Integrity's ministry. At the national level and in local chapters and diocesan networks throughout the country, the primary activities are: worship, fellowship, education, communication, outreach, and service to the church.

Metropolitan Community Church

Founded in 1968 as the first church in the world with a positive ministry to the LGBT Community, Metropolitan Community Church has been a beacon of hope for decades. MCC Congregations provide support to LGBT people, their friends, families, and allies and continue to do amazing work in communities throughout the world. Reverend Troy Perry, the founder of MCC, presented our first ever Straight for Equality in Faith Communities award in 2012.

More Light Presbyterians

Following the risen Christ, and seeking to make the Church a true community of hospitality, the mission of More Light Presbyterians is to work for the full participation of LGBT people of faith in the life, ministry and witness of the Presbyterian Church (USA).

New Ways Ministry

New Ways Ministry is an LGBTQ-positive ministry of advocacy and justice for lesbian, gay, bisexual, and transgender (LGBT) Catholics, and reconciliation within the larger Christian and civil communities.

Q Christian Fellowship

Q Christian Fellowship is a diverse community with varied backgrounds, cultures, theologies and denominations, drawn together through love of Christ and belief that every person is a beloved child of God.

Queer Theology

Supportive community and in-depth resources for queer Christians and straight supporters. Some materials are priced subscriptions.

Reconciling Ministries Network

The Reconciling Ministries Network is focused on mobilizing United Methodists of all sexual orientations and gender identities to transform our Church and world into the full expression of Christ's inclusive love.

ReconcilingWorks

Working at the intersection of oppressions, ReconcilingWorks (formerly Lutherans Concerned) embodies, inspires, advocates and organizes for the acceptance and full participation of people of all sexual orientations and gender identities within the Lutheran communion and its ecumenical and global partners.

The Reformation Project

As a Bible-based, Christian organization, The Reformation Project's mission is to advance LGBTQ inclusion in the church.

Revolution Church

Revolution was started in Phoenix, AZ in 1994 by Kelli Miller, Mike Walls and Straight for Equality in Faith Communities Honoree Jay Bakker. These three saw a desperate need within their community for the love of Christ as it was evident that the church was ignoring and even blatantly rejecting a whole subculture of people based on their appearance and lifestyle. Revolution sought to meet this need through having services that featured bands, DJs, art exhibits, a coffeehouse and guest speakers. Services are based in MSP which is where Rev. Bakker now resides.

Truth In Progress

Truth in Progress is a multi-media project dealing with issues of race, sexual orientation, and religion. We take a special look at the similar yet different experiences and histories of the Black Civil Rights and LGBT Rights Movements.

The UCC Coalition for LGBT Concerns

The Coalition provides support and sanctuary to LGBT people, their families and friends; advocates for their full inclusion in church and society; and brings Christ's affirming message of love and justice for all people. The United Church of Christ Coalition for LGBT Concerns is officially recognized by the United Church of Christ as a related, self-created organization.

Unity

A faith community for people who might call themselves spiritual but not religious. It is for those who sense the depths of their own being and celebrate the awareness of a power greater than themselves. Their mission is fully inclusive.

History of PFLAG Washburn
Washburn, Wisconsin, on the Chequamegon Bay

On February 6, 2009, a group of Chequamegon Bay area people gathered to decide if they should start a Lutherans Concerned chapter at Messiah Lutheran Church in Washburn. Lutherans Concerned (now called ReconcilingWorks) is a national, non-profit organization committed to accompanying people and ministry settings in their journey of supporting LGBTQ people. Ardys Davis, Yvette Fleming, Dianne Judd, Carri Hoagland, Nancy Hanson, Bill Luckenbill, Dick and Sandy Olson, Lois Osterberg, Don and Audrey Swedberg met at John and Cathy Odell's home.

Kathy Shattuck from Trego, Wisconsin also attended the meetings as the Lutherans Concerned representative. Kathy suggested the group consider starting a PFLAG chapter rather than a Lutherans Concerned group. As much as she believed in Lutherans Concerned, Kathy noted the group's goal of "outreach to LGBTQ people and loved ones." Since churches were not yet places of total LGBTQ support, a non-church presence might attract more people. Our group decided to start a local PFLAG chapter. The acronym PFLAG originally stood for Parents, Family, and Friends of Lesbians and Gays. Now PFLAG supports all within the LGBTQ spectrum.

PFLAG Washburn's first meeting was April 28, 2009. The movie *Prayers for Bobby* was shown at the Washburn library. Nineteen people attended. Pastor Jim Imse from Mellen attended this and almost every monthly meeting until his untimely death in 2014. Jim was known for bringing fresh flowers and known for saying, "I'm a pastor, and on behalf of all of you who have been hurt by religious messages, I apologize."

The national PFLAG organization recommends every meeting begins by stating PFLAG's vision and mission:

> *PFLAG envisions a world where diversity is celebrated and all people are respected, valued, and affirmed inclusive of their sexual orientation,*

Jocelyn Langholz

gender identity, and gender expression. PFLAG's *mission is to build on a foundation of loving families united with LGBTQ+ people and allies who support one another, and to educate ourselves and our communities, to speak up as advocates until all hearts and minds respect, value, and affirm LGBTQ+ people.*

Every time those words are said, the entire room can feel a collective sigh of relief. It feels as if people are thinking,

Ahhh, now I am with my people. I can be myself. I can open up about my loved one and know I will have support.

The original PFLAG Washburn board consisted of Nancy Hanson (president), Sandy Olson (treasurer), Dianne Judd (secretary), Bill Luckenbill and Yvette Fleming. In November of 2009 Kat Werchouski and Amy Arnao joined the board. In October of 2010 Heather Rickerl and Mary Wichita were added. Throughout the years over twelve more people have served on the PFLAG board.

A fond memory was organizing a month-long *Celebrate Diversity* art show at the Washburn Cultural Center in November, 2009, featuring an evening with singer-songwriter Sara Thomsen. Over ninety people attended the concert. PFLAG's tenth anniversary party was held at the Washburn Meditation Center with a concert by Sara who was PFLAG Washburn's 2019 Person of the year.

Throughout the years, PFLAG Washburn hosted monthly educational meetings during the school year; awarded yearly high school senior student scholarships; and selected *Persons of the Year*. Bill and Jane Luckenbill faithfully hosted the yearly summer picnic.

PFLAG Washburn held its first event during the pandemic on August 27, 2020, at the Washburn Elementary School parking lot. The *Persons-of-the-Year* gathering was a celebration of local high school *Gay-Straight Alliance* advisors. Greta Blancarte from Ashland, Cathy Smith from Bayfield and Washburn's Sarah Haughn all received a hand-knit rainbow scarf to honor their LGBTQ advocacy work within the schools.

The Divine Spark

In January of 2021, Shannon Swanstrom and Kate Stolp offered a presentation through Zoom on Mama Bears. Kate led the board through a strategic planning process in early 2021. The board gave Kate the new title, Volunteer Executive Director. From March, 2021, to October, 2023, Kate brought her nonprofit expertise to PFLAG Washburn. The group started to use PFLAG Washburn Chequamegon Bay in materials, although the official name remains PFLAG Washburn. Under Kate's leadership, community involvement expanded to work with school boards, Bayfield county board of supervisors, and Washburn city council. Kate created newsletters, wrote articles, and encouraged PFLAG volunteers to show up at area events for visibility.

The number of board members grew under Kate's leadership. PFLAG National strongly recommended term limits for chapter officers, so Nancy Hanson stepped down. Elise Kehle became the chapter president in March of 2023.

PFLAG Washburn's future looks bright as the board recently added Jocelyn Langholz, Lucas Philips and Kathleen Skoraczewski to join Elise Kehle, Mark Ricker, Jess Hall, Brian Heeringa, Colene Lee Beck Vallez, and Hans Veenendaal. View www.pflagwashburn.org to read board member bios, learn of upcoming events, and more.

In closing, read the words Jocelyn Langholz wrote about her desires when joining the board:

> *I expect mutual respect, support, and challenge in the name of always being better at affirming, including, and welcoming all. I expect PFLAG Washburn-Chequamegon Bay to continue to embrace its mission in a visible, compelling way, providing safety and community for LGBTQ folks and their families, and educating and advocating for change so that experiences of safety and authentic belonging is the rule in our world, not the exception.*

Let us all consider taking on such a pledge. In gratitude for the many who have supported PFLAG through these years,

Nancy Hanson
February, 2024

PFLAG Overview

PFLAG Washburn

PFLAG Washburn in the Chequamegon Bay provides the Chequamegon Bay community of Lake Superior with information and a safe space for LGBTQ+ individuals and their allies. We also are working to strengthen, support, and help make schools a safer and more inclusive space for LGBTQ+ youth.

The PFLAG Washburn's board of directors ensures the organization does the best work possible to achieve its mission and vision. The board of directors is the administrative and policymaking team for PFLAG Washburn.

PFLAG National

PFLAG is the nation's largest organization dedicated to uniting people who are lesbian, gay, bisexual, transgender, and queer (LGBTQ+) with their families, friends, and allies. Since 1973, its mission has been to advance equality and full societal affirmation of LGBTQ+ people through support, education, and advocacy.

PFLAG has updated its publication *Faith in our Families*, with this introduction:

> Discovering that a loved one is LGBTQ+ can pose new questions about your faith and may prompt you to re-evaluate beliefs that you previously took for granted. By using personal experiences from families of faith as well as faith leaders from a broad variety of traditions, this publication, updated in 2021, provides examples for reconciling your faith with the knowledge that a loved one is LGBTQ+, and broad resources to help you on the path.

This publication can be downloaded free at pflag.org.

While the actions of some churches give Christians a bad name when it comes to LGBTQ+ rights, others have worked for decades fighting the good fight toward inclusion for all. Doctrinal and sectarian splits make it difficult to keep score, but the organizations listed in the resources section starting on page 96 have been in it for the long haul.

What PFLAG Stands For

The policy statements below are some of the many which can be found on PFLAG'S national website: pflag.org.

Anti-Transgender Violence and Discrimination

PFLAG was the first national LGBTQ+ organization to mandate the full inclusion of people who are transgender as part of its expressed mission statement, approved by the Board of Directors in 1998.

PFLAG recognizes that in the 20+ years since approving this inclusive mission, discrimination, violence, and harm against transgender and gender-expansive people has greatly increased, with violence against transgender people – in particular Black transgender women – growing to epidemic proportions. PFLAG also recognizes that transgender people of color experience a compounded negative impact from their intersectional identities, including poverty, homelessness, unemployment, and health disparities.

PFLAG commits to supporting transgender and gender-expansive people; and to working to reduce and remove the root causes of this crisis of violence and injustice, including systemic racism, sexism, discrimination, and harassment. We are also committed to educating others and ourselves about gender identity and gender expression in order to meet unfounded fear with facts.

PFLAG will work to build communities that value transgender and gender-expansive people, and to reduce societal barriers that lead to harm, poverty and, too often, death. PFLAG will deploy its resources to listen to, engage, and bolster diverse transgender communities and the organizations that serve them, lifting up actions to increase opportunities for fair and just employment, housing, healthcare, and access to public services including law enforcement. PFLAG will also continue to educate law enforcement agencies and officers to reduce harm, and end the high rates of mistreatment, incarceration, denial of necessary medications, and physical and sexual assault in jails and prisons that transgender and gender-expansive people – especially Black transgender women – experience.

Adopted by the PFLAG National Board of Directors Nov. 15, 2019.

Censorship

PFLAG supports the right to honest, accurate, informative, and inclusive education to help every child learn and thrive. We support the right to learn about diverse topics, people, and histories, and strive to empower youth to think critically, encouraging them to make informed decisions for themselves.

PFLAG opposes censorship in communities, schools, and libraries of books or content that include discussion of LGBTQ+ identities, race or ethnicity, disabilities, or genders.

Adopted by the PFLAG National Board of Directors on March 21, 2022.

Equality

PFLAG seeks a just world in which all people receive understanding and equal acceptance and protection. PFLAG has and will continue to work to change or establish national and state legislation and policies to establish equality and to end discrimination against LGBTQ and other marginalized communities.

As bills, resolutions or ordinances are planned or introduced in Congress, states or municipalities, PFLAG will continue to work with legislative or executive branches of government to advocate for those that will help to end discrimination in all of its forms as a strong path toward equality for all. PFLAG is determined to end abusive or harmful policies, practices and legislation.

Adopted by the PFLAG National Board of Directors on March 16, 2017. Previous iterations of this were titled Legalized Discrimination and were adopted by the PFLAG Board of Directors on September 7, 1992. Revised January 15, 2001. Revised July 24, 2011. Revised March 18, 2017.

Faith Community Relationships

PFLAG National and PFLAG chapters are non-sectarian, non-denominational, and not affiliated with any particular religious institution. Although PFLAG chapter meetings may be held in buildings owned by religious communities, PFLAG chapters are not programs of – nor do they promote the religious beliefs of – those organizations. PFLAG recognizes:

1) Different religious traditions are practiced in our communities;

2) The importance of the free expression of religious beliefs, but also the freedom from such beliefs;

3) A person of faith and an LGBTQ person – or the family member of an LGBTQ person – need not be exclusive of one another;

4) People of all faiths openly and lovingly embrace the LGBTQ community;

5) Intolerance of LGBTQ people and their families is not a fair and just expression of religious faith.

Adopted by the PFLAG National Board of Directors on July 24, 2011. Revised July 8, 2017.

Introduction
to the First Edition

Welcome. The Divine Spark represents a collection of stories from LGBTQ parishoners and others who answered the question: What would I say to someone of any age, but especially to a young person who is gender non-conforming, or to a young person who is starting to notice their own same-gender attraction, upon hearing the comments:

It is against God's will to be gay.

You can pray the gay away.

Men should not wear women's clothing.

You are a girl. Stop changing who God made you to be.

Love the sinner, hate the sin.

God hates fags.

Messiah Lutheran council president Keith Holm wrote the first story. He said to me, "Just to let you know, this is a huge step for me even after all these years."

As the articles came in, I could feel their life-giving and lifesaving nature. I offer deep gratitude to each writer for their willingness to share experiences of rejection, non-acceptance, judgment, and isolation. Thank you.

Providing straight people and LGBTQ people a resource to help us promote equality serves as the principal reason for the book. Readers might also wonder what lies behind the struggle, and what

Introduction to First Edition

can people do about it. Rev. Nate Aaseng explains the error of using the Bible to deliver such wrongful pain to LGBTQ people. Rev. Dale Chesley reflects upon his spiritual growth beginning with his first days of seminary when he could not understand how women could serve as pastors because the Bible forbade it. Dale's chapter lends insight and empathy for those who learn one concept, then eventually realize another, reasonable, more compassionate view exists.

In the chapter, *The Next Step* Executive Director of ReconcilingWorks Aubrey Thonvold has enumerated ways for us to work together to increase instances of acceptance, hope, and joy for those who identify as gay, lesbian, bi-sexual, transgender, gender nonconforming, as well as for those who are questioning. ReconcilingWorks, a nonprofit organization, recognizes that racism, sexism, ageism, able-ism, heterosexism, and all other artificial distinctions seeking to advance one group's privileges and preferences over another, conspire to diminish our world and church.

Artist G. Scott Hanson designed the cover art. When asked how he came up with the image, he replied, "People are created with so much in common, yet at the same time, we are each unique." His art inspired the book's title. While reading the stories, I got the sense people are pleading, *Please see the love and light in me. Please love and accept me. God made me just as much as God made you.*

Truly a divine spark lives in all of us. Let us grow in our ability to see and celebrate the Creator's work.

Love and prayers,
Rev. Nancy Hanson

Epilogue
from the First Edition

Of the nearly 7.2 billion people on earth, about 2.2 billion call themselves Christian. Those who follow the teachings of Jesus include a very diverse group. Each sect undertakes the examination, interpretation, and application of their ancient texts, the most popular of which remains the Bible. The world's other religions comprise approximately 4 billion people. The approximately one billion people who classify as secular, nonreligious, agnostic, and atheist include a great many who consider themselves "spiritual, but not religious."

Pointedly, many of us feel some kind of spiritual tug. We want something more. We hope for an afterlife however defined. Faced with any number of sets of beliefs, we often choose someone or something to follow. In my case, largely due to my upbringing, I subscribe to Christianity. Most followers of Jesus know of His care for people on the margins.

If I am thirsty, hungry, naked, sick, a stranger, or if I am in prison, Christians are encouraged to see the face of Christ in me. LGBTQ people, however, remain the only marginalized group who

Epilogue from the First Edition

get clobbered by the Bible. Living on the margins of society already has difficult challenges. If I am poor and you use the Bible to justify walking alongside me, then I may be touched by the Jesus in your Bible. But if I am a person who is LGBTQ and you use your Bible to tell me my same-gender attraction or my desire to dress a particular way constitutes wrongfulness and sin, then what course do I have? I have to wonder about God. I have little choice but to forsake whatever such a God has to offer.

A piano teacher, a medical doctor, my cousin Chuck, deep within me I knew them only as people, nothing more, just souls trying to get from one life to the next. I often wonder, "What would it feel like to be told your natural sexual desire is sinful? An abomination? What would it feel like to be told by the most minted religious people and all their followers that I am inherently disordered?"

As a straight person not once have I heard such comments directed at me. From my first crush, I have lived within the privilege of the majority. When we become infatuated, fall in love, get engaged, married, our society views us as normal. If I am LGBTQ, however, every single step of the way in sexual attraction becomes riddled with, "What do they think of me? Do they like gay people? Can I hold hands? I'm attracted, but how can I know if this person will like me back?" Admittedly, straight people experience the latter, but without the other concerns. I am indeed a privileged heterosexual.

Having a minority sexual orientation presents many unique difficulties. One of them is that millions of "religious" people believe they know for an absolute certainty that who you are does not fit into God's plan. I cannot fathom a more wrongful teaching.

Hence, the push behind this book. Of all humanity's pie, the slice here consists of pretty much Christian and Lutheran. Even if you fall into the nonreligious category, please take the time to read and understand because we need to spread the message. If we help one person move from thoughts like: "I'm a screw up. I must be evil. Who I am does not fit. I am a freak," to thoughts like: "I am a beloved child of God who made me and loves me just as I am," then we will make our world a better, safer, and more peaceful place.

Let's do it.

Love in Christ,
Nancy Hanson
February, 2018

Acknowledgments

I acknowledge all those whose divine sparks have been shining in my life including members of First Lutheran and Messiah Lutheran Churches. They fully supported the creation of this book in 2018. It was an honor and joy to serve those two flocks. Now retired, I realize even more how many times they shepherded me instead of the other way around.

Tamarack Health Ashland Medical Center made possible the printing of this second edition through their generous grant to PFLAG Washburn.

The divine spark truly resides in everyone in a variety of ways. In both first and second editions, editor Philip Sorensen brought an attentive spark to the projects, reviewing most every word with his red pen. Mark Babel and Will Pipkin, owners of CopyThat in Ashland, gave their utmost in time and talent with design as well as content suggestions.

Amanda Forsberg, an account executive at Smartpress, handled the printing of this book with prompt professionalism.

The second edition contains new material by Mary Bondeson, Jeanne Clark, Yolanda Denson-Byers, Carri Hoagland, Keith Holm, Kate Stolp, Sorley Swanstrom-Arnold, and Michael Van Uytven. Their honest, insightful, encouraging stories make this book deeper and richer.

My friends and family are too numerous to mention by name. You know who you are and I am so thankful for you.

Thank you, all.

Nancy Hanson
February, 2024

The Divine Spark

How to Purchase
The Divine Spark

Copies of this book are available for $15 each. To place an order please write, or go to www.pflagwashburn.org. Indicate the number of books needed, include payment for the books, plus $4.00 for shipping and handling.

Make checks payable to PFLAG Washburn and mail to:

    PFLAG Washburn
    P.O. Box 434, Washburn, WI 54891

Discounts on multiple copies are available while supplies last. To inquire about discounts please call (715) 209-1100.

Copies are also available at Shepherd of the Hills Lutheran Church, 500 Blake Road South, Edina, Minnesota. To place an order, call (952) 935-3457, visit www.sothchurch.com, or email office@sothchurch.com.